UNDERSTANDING
EDWARD ALBEE

Understanding Contemporary American Literature

Matthew J. Bruccoli, *Editor*

UNDERSTANDING
Edward
ALBEE

BY MATTHEW C. ROUDANÉ

UNIVERSITY OF SOUTH CAROLINA PRESS

Copyright © University of South Carolina 1987

Published in Columbia, South Carolina, by the
University of South Carolina Press

Manufactured in the United States of America

Library of Congress Cataloging-in-Publication Data

Roudané, Matthew Charles, 1953–
  Understanding Edward Albee.

  (Understanding contemporary American literature)
  Bibliography: p.
  Includes index.
  1. Albee, Edward, 1928–   —Criticism and
interpretation.   I. Title.   II. Series.
PS3551.L25Z86   1987   812′.54   86-32633
ISBN 0-87249-502-7
ISBN 0-87249-503-5 (pbk.)

For
Susan and Nickolas

CONTENTS

EDITOR'S PREFACE

Understanding Contemporary American Literature has been planned as a series of guides or companions for students as well as good nonacademic readers. The editor and publisher perceive a need for these volumes because much of the influential contemporary literature makes special demands. Uninitiated readers encounter difficulty in approaching works that depart from the traditional forms and techniques of prose and poetry. Literature relies on conventions, but the conventions keep evolving; new writers form their own conventions—which in time may become familiar. Put simply, *UCAL* provides instruction in how to read certain contemporary writers—identifying and explicating their material, themes, use of language, point of view, structures, symbolism, and responses to experience.

The word *understanding* in the series title was deliberately chosen. Many willing readers lack an adequate understanding of how contemporary literature works; that is, what the author is attempting to express and the means by which it is conveyed. Although the criticism and analysis in the series have been aimed at a level of general accessibility, these introductory volumes are meant to be applied in conjunction with the works they cover. Thus they do not provide a substitute for the works and authors they introduce, but rather prepare the reader for more profitable literary experiences.

M. J. B.

ACKNOWLEDGMENTS

Earlier versions of chapter 6 appeared in *The The-atre Annual*; *Edward Albee: An Interview and Essays*, edited by Julian N. Wasserman; and *Journal of Evolutionary Psychology*. I am also grateful to Profes-sors Kolin and Davis, as well as Michael Sims, editor for G. K. Hall, for permission to use an earlier version of "A Monologue of Cruelty: Ed-ward Albee's *The Man Who Had Three Arms*" and excerpts from "A Playwright Speaks: An Interview with Edward Albee," which originally appeared in *Critical Essays on Edward Albee*, edited by Philip C. Kolin and J. Madison Davis (Boston: G. K. Hall, 1986). Parts of my other conversations with Ed-ward Albee originally appeared in the *Southern Humanities Review* and *RE: Artes Liberales*. I am grateful to the editors for permission to use some of that material here.

Passages from the following Albee plays re-printed by permission: *Who's Afraid of Virginia Woolf?*, Atheneum, 1962; *Tiny Alice*, Atheneum, 1965; *A Delicate Balance*, Atheneum, 1966; *Box and Quotations from Chairman Mao Tse-Tung*, Atheneum, 1969; *All Over*, Atheneum, 1971; *Seascape*, Athene-um, 1975; *Counting the Ways and Listening*, Athene-um, 1977; *The Lady from Dubuque*, Atheneum, 1980; and *The Man Who Had Three Arms*, Atheneum, forthcoming. *The Zoo Story and The American Dream*,

ACKNOWLEDGMENTS

Signet, 1960; *The Plays*, Vol. 1, Coward, McCann, and Geohegan, 1981.

The Georgia State University Research Grant Program provided partial funding for this project during the 1985–86 year. Virginia Spencer Carr, chair, Department of English, Georgia State University, saw to it that I received a reduced teaching load during a crucial phase of writing the book. I wish to thank Clyde Faulkner, Dean, College of Arts and Science, Georgia State University, for supporting my various research projects over the last four years.

Many thanks to the staff at the University of South Carolina Press for their efforts.

William J. Handy, professor of English at the University of Oregon, read an earlier version of the entire manuscript and made valuable comments throughout; I am indebted to him for his great help.

Special thanks go to two colleagues at Georgia State University: Wayne Erickson and Janet Gabler-Hover. Although both were busy with their own research, they read every page and, through their many thoughtful and intelligent comments, greatly enhanced the final manuscript. Another colleague, Thomas McHaney, made many helpful remarks regarding the first two chapters. Thanks to Leigh K. Pietschner, who proofed each page carefully.

ACKNOWLEDGMENTS

Thanks to Edward Albee, who has kindly, patiently, and frankly discussed his work with me over the last six years.

Charles and Orient Roudané know their influence on this book.

Finally, Susan Ashley, my wife, provided the kind of special warmth and support that made it possible to complete this book. In addition to suggesting revisions, she took time out from her own busy career to care for our son, Nickolas, when I most needed time to write. Her encouragement and love were constant, and she always provided a much-needed reality check.

UNDERSTANDING
EDWARD ALBEE

CHAPTER ONE

Understanding
Edward Albee

I designed *Understanding Edward Albee* to help theatergoers or readers better come to terms with one of America's most controversial dramatists, one who many have felt, especially during the 1960s, has done nothing less than reinvent the American theater. My primary concern centers on tracing Albee's artistic vision, which is essentially an affirmative existentialist world view, as reflected in selected original plays. I have omitted discussion of the adaptations mainly because Albee concedes that, whatever their merits or inadequacies, they are merely ways to polish his craft, to hone his technique, to concentrate on dramatic voice.

Reflecting the editorial goals of this series, the book is not comprehensive, but it provides a healthy sampling of Albee's major works, plays showing something of the range and versatility of his aesthetic imagination. In an ideal world one should see an Albee play live; the special kind of collective experience the audience shares with the actors and the multivalency of live theater simply cannot be reproduced fully in the text version. But the fact is that many coming to Albee for the first time do so from a generically different perspective—the play as a literary work. Perhaps many read the text as performance because, except for the debut of a new Albee play (which reaches a very small audience) and *The Zoo Story*, *The American Dream*, and *Who's Afraid of Virginia Woolf?* his plays are not staged as frequently as they once were. However, selected Albee plays are taught with some regularity in literature courses at the university level, and Albee himself points to the value of seeing and hearing the play as literature: "I would rather have a person who knows how to read a play *read* a play of mine and see a good production in his mind than see a bad production." As Albee explains, "Ideally, a superb production is to be seen, but given a bad production— well, I'd prefer a good reading anytime. You just have to learn how to read and be able to *see* and *hear* the play out loud while you are reading it." With Albee's remarks and the realization that his plays are often read as literature in mind, I have written the book so that one can use it whether approaching the text as performance or viewing the actual spectacle.

Career

Edward Albee began his writing career as a poet when he was six years old. He continued his struggle with poetry for the next twenty years, without success. Realizing his limitations as a poet—"I never felt like a poet; I felt like someone who was writing poetry"[1]—Albee today points out, with wry humor, that he turned to other genres: "I attempted the novel twice, in my teens, once when I was fourteen—a novel of some 1,800 pages—and again when I was sixteen, when my energies were either depleted or elsewhere, a second novel of only 900 pages." The form of the novel, like poetry, was not in accord with his artistic instincts. Thus, having tried his hand at poetry, the novel, the short story, Albee turned to playwriting. He wrote *Aliqueen*, a three-act sex farce, when he was twelve and, in his teens, *Schism*, a one-act piece whose protagonist, Michael Joyce, becomes alienated from Catholicism and finally from his own sense of humanity. But it was not until 1958 that Albee found his *daemon* while composing *The Zoo Story*. "Something very, very interesting happened with the writing of that play. I didn't discover suddenly that I was a playwright; I discovered that I had *been* a playwright all my life, but didn't know it because I hadn't written plays. . . . And so when I wrote *The Zoo Story*, I was able to start practicing my 'nature' fully." With this play Albee quickly established himself as an adamantine voice in contemporary American literature.

Albee was abandoned by his natural parents immediately after his birth on 12 March 1928 in Washington, D.C. Fortuitously, millionaires Reed and Frances Albee of Larchmont, New York, adopted the infant two weeks later, naming him Edward Franklin Albee III for his adoptive grandfather. Albee was thus taken in by a family with theatrical background, for his grandfather owned a profitable chain of vaudeville theaters, and as a young man Albee met such writers as Thornton Wilder and W. H. Auden, who, observing a limited degree of poetic talent in the boy, suggested he turn to playwriting.

A rebellious youth, Albee and school did not mix well. After being expelled from three preparatory schools and a military academy, Albee somehow managed to graduate from Choate, a Connecticut prep school. His two-year stay at Choate greatly influenced his literary aspirations, for he

UNDERSTANDING EDWARD ALBEE

received the kind of support that any young writer needs: his work—poems, short stories, essays, and one play—was accepted for publication in the *Choate Literary Magazine*.[2] He attended Trinity College in Connecticut, lasting only one and a half years before being asked to leave for not attending certain required classes and chapel. As Albee later reminisced, "I didn't write *Catcher in the Rye* and *End as a Man*; I lived them."[3]

After working at various odd jobs from 1948 to 1958, Albee felt "desperate" because he might not "make it" in any profession.[4] His $250-a-month trust fund, given by his grandmother, did not allay his uneasiness. Apparently out of a sense of youthful *Angst*, then, Albee once again committed himself to serious playwriting; in a self-consoling effort he penned *The Zoo Story*, a "sort of a thirtieth birthday present to myself."[5] Albee recalled in 1981 the creative process he experienced while composing what would be his first public success: "One evening, twenty-three years ago, I borrowed a hundred sheets or so of poor quality yellow typing paper from the Western Union office where I was employed as a messenger boy, brought it back to my Greenwich Village walk-up and placed it on the rickety kitchen table next to my battered nonportable typewriter. Three weeks later, some fifty sheets of yellow paper had become a play, and I had become a playwright."[6]

Over twenty plays, two Pulitzer Prizes, and numerous other dramatic accolades later, Albee rightfully stands side by side with the other major shapers of the American stage: Eugene O'Neill, Tennessee Williams, and Arthur Miller.[7]

Overview

Albee's Dramatic Theory and Art

Ever since Jerry fatally impaled himself on the knife in *The Zoo Story*, Mommy and Daddy recounted their spiritual dismemberment of their child in *The American Dream*, and George and Martha verbally assaulted each other in *Who's Afraid of Virginia Woolf?* Edward Albee has been recognized for his focus on confrontation and death. Indeed, verbal dueling and death—real and imagined, physical and psychological—pervade the Albee canon. His plays typically address such issues as betrayal, abandonment, withdrawal into a death-in-life existence—hardly issues appealing to the orthodox world of Broadway. And yet, even after reluctantly making a successful transition to the Great White Way in the early 1960s, Albee continually returns to exploring the darker side of the human soulscape.

UNDERSTANDING EDWARD ALBEE

The Albee hero and the Albee text, with disturbing frequency in the later plays, seem almost savagely divided against themselves. Given such issues and charges of self-destruction, it is hardly surprising to discover both students and critics labeling Albee a pessimistic or even nihilistic writer, a dramatist whose plays are single-mindedly fixed on presenting the demonic, the destructive. Gilbert Debusscher, for instance, concludes that "Albee's work contains no positive philosophical or social message. His theater belongs to the pessimistic, defeatist or nihilistic current which characterizes the entire contemporary theatrical scene. . . . Thus Albee suggests that from human solitude there is no exit: only death delivers us in putting an end to our conscious life."[8] Debusscher's pronouncement, voiced in 1967, characterizes much of the critical attitude regarding Albee's achievement. Further, many theatergoers or readers experiencing Albee for the first time often find him a depressing, cynical writer. Such a critical reception, coupled with Albee's alleged failings in the later plays, has made the playwright, in Robert Brustein's words, "the raw flesh of the American theater" world.[9]

But one way to understand more fully Albee's theater is to consider his world view as reflected in his thematic concerns. A careful viewer or reader will discover that the plays embody an affirmative vision of human experience, one dispelling Albee's reputation as a nihilistic dramatist. Underneath the external action, aggressive texts, and obvious preoccupation with death lies an inner drama that discloses the playwright's compassion for his fellow human beings.

This sense of compassion, this affirmative vision, becomes easier to understand when one listens to the playwright. Albee outlines what thematically engaged his imagination:

I am very concerned with the fact that so many people turn off because it is easier; that they don't stay fully aware during the course of their lives, in all the choices they make: social, economic, political, aesthetic. They turn off because it's easier. But I find that anything less than absolutely full, dangerous participation is an absolute waste of some rather valuable time. . . . I am concerned with being as self-aware, and open to all kinds of experience on its own terms—I think those conditions, given half a chance, will produce better self-government, a better society, a better everything else.[10]

Albee's observation provides a key to understanding all of the plays. Alluding to a spiritual malaise that may psychologically anesthetize the individual, Albee suggests that "full, dangerous participation" in human intercourse is a necessary correlate

UNDERSTANDING EDWARD ALBEE

to living authentically. His remarks also suggest something of his underlying hope or optimism for his fellow human beings. He agrees with Martin Heidegger in *Being and Time* that through the process of existence the individual may sculpt a "better self-government." The Albee play, in brief, becomes equipment for living. As the Woman in *Listening* recalls her grandmother saying, "We don't have to live, you know, unless we wish to; the greatest sin, no matter what they *tell* you, the greatest sin in living is doing it badly—stupidly, or as if you weren't really alive."[11] Her reflection could well serve as a touchstone of the ethical problem with which every Albee hero deals. In plays as different in dramatic conception as *The Zoo Story*, *Box*, *Quotations from Chairman Mao Tse-Tung*, and *The Man Who Had Three Arms*, Albee consistently implies that one can choose consciously to intermix the intellect and the emotions into a new whole, measured qualitatively, which is the aware individual.

While the plays appear consistent in artistic purpose, they are quite varied in method. Albee uses a wide range of theatrical styles and technical devices to present naturalistic and satiric images as well as expressionistic and absurdist images of the human predicament. The plays range from fourteen-minute sketches (*Fam and Yam*, *The Sandbox*) to

UNDERSTANDING EDWARD ALBEE

full-length Broadway productions (*Who's Afraid of Virginia Woolf? Tiny Alice*). Occasionally Albee presents social protest pieces (*The Death of Bessie Smith, The American Dream, The Man Who Had Three Arms*) or domestic dramas staging imbalances within relationships (*A Delicate Balance, All Over*). He has borrowed from others, with less than satisfying results, in the adaptations (*Malcolm, The Ballad of the Sad Cafe, Everything in the Garden, Lolita*), only to return to innovative plays whose musical quality complements the visual spectacle (*Box* and *Quotations from Chairman Mao Tse-Tung*). A technically versatile dramatist, Albee demonstrates—often at the cost of commercial if not critical success—a willingness to take aesthetic risks, a deliberate attempt to explore the boundaries, the essences of the theater. As Albee writes in his prefatory remarks to the interrelated plays *Box* and *Quotations from Chairman Mao Tse-Tung*, two of his most structurally experimental works, "Since art must move—or wither—the playwright must try to alter the forms within which his precursors have had to work."[12] Each play demonstrates Albee's ongoing efforts to reinvent dramatic language and contexts, his awareness of the modern dramatic tradition, and his individual talents. Such experiments invited Anne Paolucci to observe: "Albee's arrogance as an innovator is prompted by profound artistic instincts which are constantly at work reshaping dramatic conventions. He does not discard such conventions, but restructures them according to the organic demands of his artistic themes."[13]

In his experiments with dramaturgic boundaries he places much faith, and responsibility, in his audience. It is a faith predicated on Albee's conviction that the ideal audience approaches a play unencumbered by preconceptions or distorting labels, with the capability to suspend disbelief willingly and to immerse itself fully within the three-dimensional essence of the stage experience. Albee rejects the audience as voyeur. He courts the audience as active participant. Of course, Albee does not direct characters to assault the audience physically, as Julian Beck of the Living Theatre had performers do with his audience. But the structure and language of an Albee play conspire to assault the audience's individual and collective sensibility. As Albee explains:

In nine or ten of my plays, you'll notice, actors talk directly to the audience. In my mind, this is a way of involving the audience; of embarrassing, if need be, the audience into participation. It may have the reverse effect: some audiences don't like this; they get upset by it quite often; it may alienate them. But I am trying very hard to *involve* them. I don't like the audience as voyeur, the audience as passive spectator. I want the audience as participant. In that sense, I agree with Artaud: that sometimes we should literally draw blood. I am very fond of doing that because voyeurism in the theater lets people off the hook.[14]

Albee's reference to the French actor, director, and aesthetician Antonin Artaud is important. In 1938 Artaud, founder of the Theater of Cruelty, wrote *The Theatre and Its Double*, a study which Robert Brustein calls "one of the most influential, as well as one of the most inflammatory, documents of our time."[15] In this seminal study Artaud discusses, among many other issues, the civic function of the theater: the dramatic experience should "disturb the senses' repose," should unleash "the repressed unconscious," should produce "a virtual revolt."[16] Cruelty, for Artaud, was the primary ingredient that could generate an apocalyptic revolt within the audience—an audience which Artaud viewed as the bourgeois Parisian who expected realistic performances. But it is important to recognize that his theories extolling aggression and violence were grounded more in the cerebral and metaphysical than in the merely physical. His aesthetic imagination focused on religious, metaphysical experiences. "Artaud sought to make it clear that the cruelty he had in mind was

UNDERSTANDING EDWARD ALBEE

not brutal and sadistic but cosmic and metaphysical," writes Naomi Greene in *Antonin Artaud: Poet Without Words*; "the task of the theater, he maintained, is to show that life itself is cruel because metaphysical forces are constantly at work to deprive man of his freedom."[17] Albee, of course, does not stage the kind of theater Artaud envisioned: he would seem too conventional, too conservative, too reliant on language (despite his distrust of language in the later plays) for Artaud. But Artaud's influence on Albee is unmistakable in terms of the use of physical, psychological, and metaphysical violence on the stage. Two years later, again referring to Artaud's influence on his own work, Albee emphasized the value of staging militant performances:

All drama goes for blood in one way or another. Some drama, which contains itself behind the invisible fourth wall, does it by giving the audience the illusion that it is the spectator. This isn't always true: if the drama succeeds the audience is *bloodied*, but in a different way. And sometimes the act of aggression is direct or indirect, but it is always an act of aggression. And this is why I try very hard to involve the audience. As I've mentioned to you before, I want the audience to participate in the dramatic experience.[18]

Albee's theatrical strategy ideally minimizes the actor/audience barrier. As Paolucci, writing fourteen years after her influential study of Albee's theater, argues, "What makes Albee stand out . . . is his insistence on giving us the Pirandellian sense of realism on stage, drawing us into the play and slowly pulling away the scaffolding that separates us from the core of the experience, casting us as participants in the drama."[19] As active participants within the play the audience contributes to the ritualized forms of confrontation and expiation that characterize much of Albee's work. This is why Albee sees the violence and death as, finally, and paradoxically enough, life-giving:

If one approaches the theater in a state of innocence, sober, without preconceptions, and willing to partici- pate; if they are willing to have the status quo assaulted; if they're willing to have their conscious- ness raised, their values questioned—or reaffirmed; if they are willing to understand that the theater is a live and dangerous experience—and therefore a *life-giving force*—then perhaps they are approaching the theater in an ideal state and that's the audience I wish I were writing for.[20]

Albee animates his "life-giving" theater through language. In fact, language stands as the most conspicuous feature of his dramaturgy as well as his major contribution to American drama. Albee's verbal duels, some of which seem analo- gous to musical arias, are now a well-known part

UNDERSTANDING EDWARD ALBEE

of American dramatic history. In both text and performance his technical virtuosity emanates from an ability to capture the values, personal politics, and often limited perceptions of his characters through language. "The accusative dialogue, and its cruelties" in *Who's Afraid of Virginia Woolf?* contends Ruby Cohn, "are the wittiest ever heard on the American stage."[21] Similarly, C. W. E. Bigsby characterizes Albee's work thus: "By turns witty and abrasive, and with a control over language, its rhythms and nuances, unmatched in the American theater, he broke new ground with each play, refusing to repeat his early Broadway success."[22] Although the language from *A Delicate Balance* onward becomes, as Thomas P. Adler argues, more stylized, elliptical, even "pretentious and obscure,"[23] Albee's repartee—when he is at his best—still generates a compelling energy within each play. One of the chief tenets of the Living Theatre, writes Julian Beck, was to "revivify language," and through language the playwright might realize the civic and religious powers of the art of drama: *"to increase conscious awareness, to stress the sacredness of life, to break down the walls."*[24] Although Albee was in no way associated with the Living Theatre, the language of his early plays captured the "kinetic" energy which

Judith Malina and Beck felt so necessary for the stage.

Just as Albee is quite varied in his use of language, so the critics are quite varied in their interpretations of the plays. Some scholars analyze Albee within a historical context while others concentrate on psychohistories of the characters.[25] Some read the plays from a biographical perspective, arguing that Albee's strained relations with his parents during his youth and his homosexuality find expression through the sexual tensions in the plays;[26] others see Albee as primarily a social protester.[27] Such volumes as Philip C. Kolin and J. Madison Davis's *Critical Essays on Edward Albee* reflect the enormous variety of interpretations which the plays absorb.[28] Add to the list of books on Albee the over 1,200 articles on the plays and it is no wonder that Albee students and scholars may be more confused by the criticism than by the dramas.

Albee's theater, for many, reflects the sweep and play of a nation thinking in front of itself, of a culture seeking to locate its identity through the ritualized action implicit in the art of theater. Albee, it seemed, was the new Angry Young Man, a decidedly sociopolitical dramatist who anticipated, and subsequently became a part of, the social eruptions in the United States during the

UNDERSTANDING EDWARD ALBEE

1960s. Such a play as *The Death of Bessie Smith* only cemented his reputation as a "political" writer, one whose rage existed in equipoise with his moral seriousness. But to regard *The Death of Bessie Smith* as a thesis play, a play about racism, a social protest piece, does not fully account for its power. Such an assessment is not meant to discount the political dimensions of the play; clearly it tackles racism, one of America's most controversial social, historical, and moral issues. But the play's real subject lies less in its analysis of bigotry and prejudice than in its treatment of internal forces—psychological, ethical, spiritual—which negate the possibility of the individual coming to terms with the self. *The Death of Bessie Smith*, more than pinpointing a broader social malaise, charts private crimes of the heart. The Nurse's outburst near the end of the play bodies forth the existential experience, a kind of sickness unto death, confronting all the characters:

I am *sick*. I am sick of everything in this hot, stupid, fly-ridden *world*. I am sick of the disparity between things as they are, and as they should be! I am sick of this desk . . . this uniform . . . it scratches . . . I am sick of the sight of *you* . . . the *thought* of you makes me . . . *itch* . . . I am sick of *him*. (*Soft now: a chant*) I am sick of talking to people on the phone in this damn stupid hospital. . . . I am sick of the smell of

Lysol . . . I could die of it. . . . I am sick of going to bed and I am sick of waking up. . . . I am tired . . . I am tired of the truth . . . and I am tired of lying about the truth . . . I am tired of my skin. . . . I WANT OUT![29]

The Nurse's is a kind of ontological sickness, a world-weariness which precipitates her violent attacks, defensiveness, sense of entrapment. The Nurse's condition is emblematic of the kind of frustration and self-betrayal afflicting the Intern and the Orderly. Bessie Smith clearly is a victim of racial hatred. But to Albee the Nurse, the Intern, and the Orderly must also be seen as victims, individuals unable to accept personal and social responsibilities that go with being human.

Despite his experiments with dramatic language and structure, and such seemingly political works as *The Death of Bessie Smith*, Albee presents a kind of intuitive *existentialist* apprehension of experience. When Albee was in his teens, reading the works of Albert Camus, he probably read in *The Rebel* that "the subject matter of art has been extended from psychology to the human condition."[30] The human condition becomes the nerve center of each play, an unmistakable thematic dimension of Albee's vision. His vision is testimony to, as Hazel E. Barnes argued in her study of existentialism and literature, "the ways whereby

UNDERSTANDING EDWARD ALBEE

men and women either seek in bad faith to avoid the responsibilities which go with being human, or find the courage to recognize and 'engage' their freedom."[31] Throughout his career, in plays, college lectures, and private conversations, Albee alludes to the influence the existentialist movement exerts on his artistic vision. In an early interview, for instance, he discussed the impact of the existentialist movement on the literary artist:

The existentialist and post-existentialist revaluation of the nature of reality and what everything is about in man's position to it came shortly after the 2nd World War. I don't think that it is an accident that it gained the importance in writers' minds that it has now as a result of the bomb at Hiroshima. We developed the possibility of destroying ourselves totally and completely in a second. The ideals, the totems, the panaceas don't work much anymore and the whole concept of absurdity is a great deal less absurd now than it was before about 1945.[32]

Such a "revaluation of the nature of reality," particularly within an existentialist context, has since become the unifying principle within Albee's aesthetic. Over two decades later he reaffirms the existentialist texture of his theater, focusing on what for him stands as the most compelling subject, consciousness:

The single journey through consciousness should be

participated in as fully as possible by the individual, no matter how dangerous or cruel or terror-filled that experience may be. We only go through it once, unless the agnostics are proved wrong, and so we must do it fully conscious. One of the things art does is to not let people sleep their way through their lives. If the universe makes no sense, well perhaps we, the individual, can make sense of the cosmos. We must go on, we must not add to the chaos but deal honestly with the idea of order, whether it is arbitrary or not. As all of my plays suggest, so many people prefer to go through their lives semiconscious and they end up in a terrible panic because they've wasted so much. But being as self-aware, as awake, as open to various experience will produce a better society and a more intelligent self-government.[33]

The confluence of public issues and private tensions—the civic as well as personal functions of the theater—is wedded to Albee's sense of consciousness. The preeminence of consciousness necessarily generates within his heroes primal anxieties, dissociations, imbalances. Certainties yield to ambivalences. If his heroes demonstrate gracelessness under pressure, if their deadening routines prompt lifelong friends to respond to each other as uninvited guests, Albee still maintains faith in the regenerative powers of the human imagination. Animating the imaginative faculties, of course, is consciousness, and Albee celebrates Albert Camus's views concerning self-awareness.

UNDERSTANDING EDWARD ALBEE

"Weariness comes at the end of the acts of a mechanical life," writes Camus in *The Myth of Sisyphus*, "but at the same time it inaugurates the impulse to consciousness. It awakens consciousness and provokes what follows. . . . For everything begins with consciousness and nothing is worth anything except through it."[34]

Physical, psychological, and spiritual forces—these stand as the elements that so often converge within Albee's characters. Such an intermixture, moreover, precipitates an elemental anxiety, what Albee calls "a personal, private yowl" that "has something to do with the anguish of us all."[35] Accordingly, the power of Albee's plays emanates not from their philosophical content or structural innovations, but from their "artistic" texture that dramatizes man's struggle with the complex and messy business of living. If his heroes are to "burst the spirit's sleep," as Saul Bellow writes in *Henderson the Rain King*,[36] such epiphanic moments are not realized through the process of philosophic intellection but, as Bellow's hero discovers, through the process of concrete immersion into a cosmos which seems exciting yet hostile, reliable yet puckish, life-giving yet death-saturated.

Albee's experiments with dramatic form and his thematic unity at times place him within a postmodern movement; but if one considers the body of his dramatic work as a whole, the playwright harkens back to the Romantic tradition. Like Saul Bellow and Bernard Malamud, Albee believes in the talismanic powers of the aesthetic imagination and art to liberate, to create a liberal humanism. Underneath his characters' public bravado lies an ongoing inner drama, a subtext presenting characters' quest for consciousness. The profound irony stems from the characters' inability to understand the regenerative power of consciousness.

For Albee the play becomes the hour of consciousness. During this fleeting but illuminating hour Albee's affirmative vision underscores the importance of confronting one's self and the other, without O'Neill's "pipe dreams" or illusions. Further, his vision recognizes the benefit of regenerating the individual's spirit. Albee, in short, believes in the value and dignity of man. In the midst of dehumanizing society his heroes, perhaps irrationally, affirm living. If O'Neill's, Ionesco's, Mamet's, or Beckett's characters seem aware of suffering, they also accept an attitude that precludes any significant growth. In contrast, Albee's heroes suffer, dwell in an absurd world, but realize the opportunity for growth and change. They often experience a coming to consciousness that draws them—to allude to an important metaphor in *Who's*

UNDERSTANDING EDWARD ALBEE

Afraid of Virginia Woolf?—toward "the marrow": toward the essence, the core of their relationships. Stripped of illusions, Albee's protagonists stand naked. And once naked, they begin rekindling those forces which may profoundly alter their stance towards human encounters. Of course, Albee offers no guarantee of order, comprehension, survival, or love. Whether each character takes advantage of powers of consciousness varies from play to play, but the point remains fixed: Albee's theater consistently stages the *possibility* that his heroes, and perhaps the audience, through the process of engagement can become more honest with both their inner and outer worlds.

Therefore, to regard Albee's use of verbal dueling and death as proof of a pessimistic vision—as many Albeephiles and Albeephobes have done—is misleading. Throughout his career, Albee defines in dramatic terms, to use his own words, "how we lie to ourselves and to each other, how we try to live without the cleansing consciousness of death."[37] To experience the "cleansing" effects of such self-awareness, the Albee hero necessarily questions the nature of his or her values, predicaments, and relationships. To live honestly—as Jerry in *The Zoo Story* and Grandma in *The Sandbox* and George and Martha in *Who's Afraid of Virginia Woolf?* and Tobias in *A Delicate Balance* and the Wife in *All Over* and Charlie in *Seascape* and Jo in *The Lady from Dubuque* and Himself in *The Man Who Had Three Arms* discover—is a liberating quality that frees the mind, even at the risk of facing a grimly deterministic world in which one suddenly feels the utter precariousness of existence. That certain characters fail to take advantage of this capacity to bear a world so conceived, that certain audiences seem unwilling to accept experiments with dramatic language and structure, that sometimes the plays themselves cannot always sustain the dramaturgic burdens placed upon them, does not negate the significance, Albee suggests throughout his theater, of such self-perception.

Notes

1. Edward Albee, public lecture, Georgia State University, Atlanta, 31 Oct. 1985. All subsequent biographical remarks are from this lecture unless otherwise noted.

2. C. W. E. Bigsby discusses the impact of Albee's early work in *Introduction to Twentieth-Century American Drama* (New York: Cambridge University Press, 1984) 2: 251–256.

3. Walter Wager, ed., *The Playwrights Speak* (New York: Delta, 1968) 27.

4. Richard E. Amacher, *Edward Albee*, rev. ed. (Boston: Twayne, 1982) 5.

5. Wager 40.

6. Edward Albee, *The Plays* (New York: Coward, McCann, and Geohegan, 1981) 1:7.

7. Biographical details on Albee remain skimpy; there is no biography, and Albee tries to avoid talking about his past and present home life. However, the following sources contain useful information: Amacher 1–12; Bigsby 249–56; Thomas B. Morgan, "Angry Playwright in a Soft Spell," *Life* (26 May 1967); Barbara La Fontaine, "Triple Threat On, Off and Off-Off Broadway," *New York Times Magazine* 25 Feb. 1968: 36–37, 39–40, 42, 44, 46. Martha Smilgis, "Edward Albee Blames His Newest Broadway Flop on the Critics and Casts for *Lolita* on Subways," *People* 25 Feb. 1980: 70, 73; Wager 25–67.

8. Gilbert Debusscher, *Edward Albee: Tradition and Renewal*, trans. Anne D. Williams (Brussels: Center for American Studies, 1967) 82.

9. Robert Brustein, "Self-Parody and Self-Murder," *New Republic* Mar. 1980: 26.

10. Matthew C. Roudané, "An Interview with Edward Albee," *Southern Humanities Review* 16 (1982): 41, 43.

11. Edward Albee, *Counting the Ways and Listening* (New York: Atheneum, 1977) 110.

12. Edward Albee, *Box and Quotations from Chairman Mao Tse-Tung* (New York: Atheneum, 1969) x.

13. Anne Paolucci, *From Tension to Tonic: The Plays of Edward Albee* (Carbondale: Southern Illinois University Press, 1972) 4.

14. Matthew C. Roudané, "Albee on Albee," *RE: Artes Liberales* 10 (1984): 1.

15. Robert Brustein, *The Theatre of Revolt* (Boston: Little, Brown, 1964) 363.

16. Antonin Artaud, *The Theatre and Its Double*, trans. Mary Caroline Richards (New York: Grove, 1958) 41.

17. Naomi Greene, *Antonin Artaud: Poet Without Words* (New York: Simon and Schuster, 1970) 117.

18. Matthew C. Roudané, "A Playwright Speaks: An Interview with Edward Albee," *Critical Essays on Edward Albee* ed. Philip C. Kolin and J. Madison Davis (Boston: Hall, 1986) 195.

19. Anne Paolucci, "Albee and the Restructuring of the Modern Stage," *Studies in American Drama, 1945–Present* 1 (1986): 11.

20. Roudané, "A Playwright Speaks" 194.

21. Ruby Cohn, *Currents in Contemporary Drama* (Bloomington: Indiana University Press, 1969) 72.

22. Bigsby 327.

23. Thomas P. Adler, "Art or Craft: Language in the Plays of Albee's Second Decade," *Edward Albee: Planned Wilderness*, ed. Patricia De La Fuente (Edinburg, TX; Pan American University Press, 1980) 45.

24. Julian Beck, "Storming the Barricades," Kenneth H. Brown, *The Brig* (New York: Hill and Wang, 1965) 7, 9, 18.

25. See Debusscher; C. W. E. Bigsby, *Edward Albee* (Edinburgh: Oliver and Boyd, 1969); and Anita Marie Stenz, *Edward Albee: The Poet of Loss* (The Hague: Mounton, 1978).

26. See Foster Hirsch, *Who's Afraid of Edward Albee?* (Berkeley: Creative Arts, 1978).

27. See Ruby Cohn, *Edward Albee* (Minneapolis: University of Minnesota Press, 1969); Michael E. Rutenberg, *Edward Albee: Playwright in Protest* (New York: Avon, 1969); and Gerald McCarthy, *Edward Albee* (London: Macmillan, 1985).

28. See the introduction, *Critical Essays on Edward Albee*, which provides an excellent bibliographic essay covering Albee scholarship through 1985.

29. Albee, *The Plays* 1:116.

30. Albee has repeatedly said that Camus greatly influenced his dramaturgy. See, for example, "Edward Albee: An Interview," in De La Fuente 6; and Roudané, "An Interview with Edward Albee" 42.

31. Hazel E. Barnes, *Humanistic Existentialism: The Literature of Possibility* (Lincoln: University of Nebraska Press, 1959) 10.

32. Digby Diehl, "Edward Albee," *Transatlantic Review* 13 (1963): 72.

33. Roudané, "A Playwright Speaks" 198.

34. Albert Camus, *The Myth of Sisyphus and Other Essays* (New York: Vintage, 1955) 10.

35. Edward Albee, *The Zoo Story and The American Dream* (New York: Signet, 1960) 54.

36. Saul Bellow, *Henderson the Rain King* (Greenwich, CN.: Fawcett Crest, 1959) 68.

37. Albee, *The Plays* 1: 10.

CHAPTER TWO

Beginnings: *The Zoo Story* and *The American Dream*

The Zoo Story

"When I wrote the play . . . I was making a living delivering telegrams, and I did quite a bit of walking. I was always delivering telegrams to people living in rooming houses. I met all those people in the play in rooming houses. Jerry, the hero, is still around. He changes his shape from year to year." In 1974 Albee thus described *The Zoo Story*, first produced at the Schiller Theater Werkstatt, West Berlin, Germany, on 28 September 1959. The play embodies many of the qualities that have since come to characterize vintage Albee. The necessity of ritualized confrontation, the primacy of communication, the paradoxical mixture of love and hate, the cleverly abrasive dialogue, the religious and political textures, the tragic force of abandonment and death, the felt awareness of a gulf between the way things are and the way things could be, and the penalty of consciousness all coalesce in Albee's first and in many respects most successful composition. The play remains an exemplary achievement, one reflecting what John Barth identifies as "passionate virtuosity," the writer's ideal fusion of intellect and emotion.[1] Perhaps the most remarkable feature of *The Zoo Story* is its compelling presentation of a particular series of events which suddenly broaden to encompass universal experiences: Jerry and Peter emerge as essentially tragic figures, in the specifics of whose confrontation Albee sets forth nothing less than the general tragedy of modern existence itself.

Albee generates much of the play's tragic tension by yoking opposites together. Peter, the passive listener, lives on the East Side of New York City, and his world seems conspicuously well ordered. He represents the successful, businessman, the contented, comfortable, upper-middle-class family man. Few issues bother Peter because he shuts out any experience that might upset his cushioned life. On the other hand, Jerry is the active speaker, lives on the West Side, and his world is unquestionably fragmented. He appears as the battle-fatigued, alienated cosmic waif, the loner who searches for meaning within public issues and private values which seemingly negate themselves. Moreover, the sociopolitical dimensions of the play seemed to cast Albee as a consummate civic protester, a playfully demonic social jester, the new angry young playwright blasting societal schisms which separate the haves from the have-nots. Finally an American playwright had arrived whose aesthetic instincts existed in equipoise with his political impulses, something audiences were accustomed to expect in such great continental works as Bertoldt Brecht's *Mother Courage* or Jean Genet's *The Balcony*, for instance. Not since Elmer Rice's *The Adding Machine, Street Scene,* and *We, the People* and Robert E. Sherwood's *Idiot's Delight;* not since Clifford Odets's *Till the Day I Die, Awake and Sing!* and *Waiting for Lefty* and Arthur Miller's *All My Sons*—productions spanning from the late 1920s through the late 1940s—had the American stage witnessed such a bold social protest drama as *The Zoo Story.* And yet, while *The Zoo Story* clearly invites sociopolitical analysis, its real emphasis lies elsewhere: Albee focuses much more on the inner reality of Peter and Jerry, on the quality of their respective sensibilities, and on the existentialist choices each person makes. Albee's interest is in fundamental human values as objectified through the individual. Crimes of the heart, not the state, stand out in *The Zoo Story.*

Albee accentuates Peter and Jerry's differing

sensibilities by contrasting their worlds. Peter's world is comfortable. A publishing executive, he is married, has two daughters, pets, and a fashionable home. Every aspect of Peter's well-ordered environment seems predictable, safe. Lacking individuality and cast as the conformist in an Eisenhower era, Peter "blends perfectly into the brightly-packaged emptiness of the modern landscape."[2] Conditioned by a culture prizing language largely devoid of genuine meaning, Peter reduces external experience to prescribed formulas, unconscious that he substitutes derivative thought for original insight. Peter's world is much like that of Tolstoy's Ivan Ilych, whose life was "most simple and most ordinary and therefore most terrible."[3] Perhaps Anne Paolucci best captures the quality of Peter's consciousness, observing that he moves "monotonously on the surface of life, pushed on by a kind of inertia which is mistaken for intention."[4] Although Peter is a thinly sketched figure, as Albee admits,[5] his presence is vital because he acts as a foil. With his utterly banal responses and attendant emotional paralysis Peter accentuates Jerry's frenetic stage movements and dialogue/monologue. Peter emerges as an emblematic figure, the representative of an upper-middle-class world which Albee will assault often throughout his career. Finally, the audience is struck by the

BEGINNINGS

actionlessness of Peter's life, a point Albee reinforces not only through dialogue but through stage
descriptions as well: "A man in his early forties,
neither fat nor gaunt, neither handsome nor
homely."[6] By describing Peter in negatives, Albee
suggests much about Peter's nonparticipatory
stance toward any meaningful human encounter.
Like Tobias in *A Delicate Balance* and Charlie in
Seascape, Peter prefers to withdraw from confrontation, engagement—indeed any form of communication predicated on honest commitment. This is
why, until physically (and, by extension, morally)
pushed regarding the park bench, Peter tries
avoiding Jerry, a strategy of avoidance that occurs
on a verbal as well as nonverbal plane. Peter's
body gestures—the constant turning away during
the opening exchanges, the pretending not to hear,
raising a hand to object, the winces, the forced
smile—serve as ways of deflecting social engagement. Jerry, of course, challenges such an attitude.

Jerry's world is troubled, an environment
filled with suffering humanity and with a disarming mixture of love, hate, and squalor. His neigh-
bors—a "colored queen" who plucks his eye-
brows, the Puerto Rican family, the invisible crying
woman, the landlady—function as constant re-
minders of those whose lives are ontologically
different from Peter's. In many respects Jerry's

present environment is merely a terrible extension of his past world: his mother ran away, had numerous affairs, and wound up dead; soon after, a city bus crushed his drunken father; Jerry then moved in with his aunt, only to witness her death on his high school graduation day. Emotionally buffeted in his youth, Jerry feels abandoned on all fronts, any youthful innocence or opportunity for community subverted by a naturalistic universe. His present condition offers little sense of resolution, boundaries, solace. In fact, Jerry's relentless questions, the rapidity of speech, the quickness of breath, reveal a man in the midst of emotional collapse during what turns out to be the last hour of his life. His hypnotic overacting plainly suggests a man on the brink of madness.

For Jerry, however, near-insanity nurtures lucidity. His baffling remark—"sometimes a person has to go a very long distance out of his way to come back a short distance correctly" (21)—throws telling light on his confrontations with an unsuspecting Peter. For one perversely expiative scene, when Jerry sacrifices himself on the knife for Peter's sake, Jerry finds meaning to his existence through the ultimate form of communication: death. He has taken thirty-odd years to experience a minute of fulfillment, a tragic point where, for once, he has not depended on the kindness or

cruelty of stangers—or dogs or pornographic playing cards—but has helped another human being.
When Jerry impales himself, he has finally "come
back a short distance correctly." "Peter's made too
many safe choices far too early in his life," Albee
has remarked, "and Jerry has to shock him into
understanding the tragic sense of being alive."[7]

Because he possesses an acute insight into his
own condition, Jerry is capable of elevating a
merely pathetic situation to the tragic and, through
the catharsis of tragedy, is able to find some
coherence in what hitherto has been a meaningless
existence. Such an elevation is not present in the
works of, for instance, O'Neill. A figure such as
Yank in *The Hairy Ape* struggles to understand his
place in an industralized, dehumanizing cosmos,
but he ultimately never changes. O'Neill presents a
Yank who, from the opening curtain to scene 8,
remains caught within the dismal patterns of life,
one who remains the same: a pathetic naturalistic
victim, an object among objects, a bothersome
stoker symbolizing the helplessness of those
trapped within a grimly deterministic universe.
The play's closing image, set at the zoo where the
gorilla crushes an utterly bewildered Yank, confirms the tragic legacy of Yank's noble yet ineffectual struggle "to belong." In such plays as *Desire
Under the Elms*, *Long Day's Journey into Night*, and

The Iceman Cometh, O'Neill told the truth as he felt it: that the individual is victimized by his hubris as well as by a cajoling, beguiling external world which promotes a reliance on illusions as the only way to cope with life's absurdities and personal betrayals. Albee, beginning with Jerry in *The Zoo Story*, rejects O'Neill's vision.

In fact, Albee goes beyond the visions of his two greatest American contemporaries after O'Neill, Arthur Miller and Tennessee Williams. Despite whatever essentially Romantic tendencies that can be detected in such masterworks as *Death of a Salesman* or *A Streetcar Named Desire*, both Miller and Williams, like O'Neill before them, relied on a naturalistic vision of experience as the broader social and psychological canvas on which they placed their characters' struggles. Albee, of course, does not deny the presence of the naturalistic universe; indeed, *The Zoo Story* and *The Death of Bessie Smith* show an Albee acutely aware of the pervasive influence of a Zolaesque world. Albee retains the buffeting forces of naturalism within his imaginative terrain, but he also gives his characters the opportunity to transcend the limitations and horrors of naturalism. Jerry's and Peter's sense of consciousness ultimately enables them to go beyond Willy Loman's or Blanche Dubois's worlds.

Despite the degree of heightened awareness

BEGINNINGS

Albee bestows on Peter and Jerry, and despite the obviously contrasting realities of the two, Albee presents them as *sharing* a profound sense of isolation. This is why, in part, *The Zoo Story* stands as a kind of intuitive existentialist play. The forced communication between the two characters underscores the point. Peter fails in human intercourse because of a withdrawal into a comfortable, bourgeois life, a life denying the tragic. Legally Peter will not be accountable for Jerry's death, but, Albee implies, after this Sunday afternoon's events he will feel accountable in a spiritual sense. Peter will no longer be able to remain isolated. Jerry fails because of his inability to maintain lasting relationships in his world, a world that courts the tragic. Accountability means little to Jerry, for he would rather die than perpetuate his desperate life. Thus both characters' experiences of isolation, although prompted by seemingly opposite predicaments— Jerry is too aware of felt isolation, Peter too anesthetized to discern separateness—dovetail within a broader context of existential aloneness.

Jerry violates Peter's isolation through communication. Exceeding the limits of expected propriety for a chance first encounter, Jerry bombards Peter with a disarmingly shrill and frank account of his private life. But he does this because Peter's initial indifference prompts Jerry to rely on the powers of invention, the weaving together of fact and fiction, a method of sorting through his fragmented experience and keeping Peter transfixed. C. W. E. Bigsby makes a useful point regarding Jerry's inventiveness: "When simple conversation is subverted by Peter's inability to engage in language on any but the most superficial level, he resorts to parable, telling the story of his relationship with his landlady's dog, a relationship which parallels that between Peter and himself."[8] Jerry's often hilarious parable about the dog reveals an active, if confused, mind, a consciousness eminently capable of self-awareness and eagerly willing to make "contact" (35). While Peter has not succumbed to a willful surrendering of the spirit to the extent certain future Albee protagonists shall, his initially indifferent responses to Jerry nonetheless imply that, at least on an unconscious plane, his ethical judgments have been dulled by a withdrawal from any experience that does not fit within his limited set of values. Jerry, on the other hand, rebels against those very patterns of withdrawal. Although obviously in a different fictional context, Jerry's lovingly hateful stance toward Peter is prompted by precisely that sense of the excluding other, by those who ostracize the Jerrys of the world.

The public and private schism dividing Jerry's

world from Peter's is terribly confirmed in the dog story. Albee established his technical virtuosity, an uncanny ability to weave the tragic and the comic, in the well-known story within a play, which Jerry titles "THE STORY OF JERRY AND THE DOG!" (30). The passage, inspired partially by Tennessee Williams's *Suddenly Last Summer*,[9] is the nerve center of the play. The passage not only violates Peter's enameled self but allows Jerry the chance to clarify the nature of his self-torment, a necessary clarification which prepares him for death. The story within a play also allows the audience to view Jerry in a broader context, as something more than a neurotic misanthrope, for we see him emerging as a complex antihero. The dog parable, in symbolic terms, serves as Jerry's paradigm for the entire human situation, its intensely private narrative expanding to include a lament for all suffering humanity. With the dog story, moreover, Jerry becomes an artist. In presenting a "factual" account of his sordid past, Jerry creates a "fiction" rivaling, perhaps surpassing, objective circumstances. His imaginative faculties enable him to blur the distinctions between fact and fiction while also, as Shelly Fisher Fishkin argues, enabling "the reader to see more clearly" facts presented as fiction.[10] Although it is never known if Jerry's account of his past life is accurate, the audience has little reason to doubt its veracity. But the exactitude of his story's content becomes irrelevant; of concern is what Jerry's fictional account reveals about his present physical, psychological, and spiritual makeup. In the dog story, Jerry's mimeticism, his fiction-making power, highlights the quality of his sensibility and his desperate condition.

Rejected by family and all others, Jerry enters into a relationship with the dog, for "where better to make a beginning . . . to understand and just possibly be understood . . . a beginning of an understanding, than with . . . (*Here Jerry seems to fall into almost grotesque fatigue*) . . . than with A DOG" (35). Unlike people the dog was not indifferent: he stalked; he attacked. Through a relationship with the dog Jerry gains some insight into the paradoxical links between love and hate that will plague so many future Albee heroes: "I have learned that neither kindness nor cruelty by themselves, independent of each other, creates any effect beyond themselves; and I have learned that the two combined, together, at the same time, are the teaching emotion" (35–36). The "teaching emotion" will find its full expression only through Jerry's ritualistic murder/suicide.

Jerry uses Peter as an emotional sounding board largely because he senses the pervasive lack of communication and felt sense of estrangement

BEGINNINGS

entrapping the individual in a "zoo," the shaping
metaphor of the play. As Jerry explains:

I went to the zoo to find out more about the way people exist with animals, and the way animals exist with
each other, and with people too. It probably wasn't a
fair test, what with everyone separated by bars from
everyone else, the animals for the most part from each
other, and always the people from the animals. But, if
it's a zoo, that's the way it is (39–40).

As the shaping metaphor the zoo, with its bars and
cages, symbolizes the disconnectedness of one
human being from another which fuels Jerry's
Angst. Like the fence in Frost's "Mending Wall,"
the cages function, not as a social gathering place,
but as psychological dividers between people, the
effectively convenient separators severing meaningful encounters. Brian Way is right when he
suggests, "The entire human condition, for Jerry,
is a zoo of people (and animals) forever separated
by bars. Jerry, of course, seeks to break down the
bars and cages which keep Peter, his family, and
those like them isolated in their '*own* little zoos.' "[11]
Despite the accuracy of Jerry's lover's quarrel
with the world, Peter rejects his reasoning. But in
rejecting a thinly disguised plea for contact Peter
rejects not only a crazed man but, Albee suggests,
all experience associated with the visceral, mysterious, nonrational. Representing a consciousness

unwilling to reexamine one's milieu, Peter cannot understand or accept those like Jerry, as his outburst indicates: "I DON'T WANT TO HEAR ANY MORE" (37). Sensing Peter's rejection—not of the bizarre content of the dog story but of what he is, his total *being*—Jerry feels compelled to escalate his assault. Here Albee strengthens the parallels between Jerry's encounters with the dog and with Peter. For example, as Jerry and the dog challenged each other over territory, the entrance to the rooming house, so Jerry and Peter battle over territory, the park bench. As the dog tried to keep Jerry from his world, so Peter tries to screen Jerry from his. Finally, as Jerry and the dog engaged in physical skirmishes, so the tension between the two men builds, the tragic and comic uniting:

> *Peter (Furious)*: Look, you; get off my bench. I don't care if it makes any sense or not. I want this bench to myself; I want you OFF IT!
> *Jerry (Mocking)*: Aw . . . look who's mad.
> *Peter*: GET OUT!
> *Jerry*: No.
> *Peter*: I WARN YOU!
> *Jerry*: Do you know how ridiculous you look *now*?
> *Peter (His fury and self-consciousness have possessed him)*: It doesn't matter. (*He is almost crying*) GET AWAY FROM MY BENCH! (44)

As with so many of Albee's subsequent plays, *The*

BEGINNINGS

Zoo Story stages a profound sense of engagement between two individuals, a felt militancy between characters that precedes the cathartic ending. From this point onward Peter appears aroused, angered, ready to define himself through concrete deeds rather than false compromises. Within the closing febrile scenes of the play Peter experiences Camus's "definitive awakening,"[12] a moment in which he comes to consciousness wherein he can apprehend the world external to the self in qualitatively new terms.

When he impales himself on the knife, Jerry not only gains his expiation but also shatters all of Peter's predictable patterns. Face to face, Jerry forces Peter into the "contact" he seeks throughout the play. Jerry finds his ultimate mode of engagement and communication; but paradoxically, it is the knife that gives meaning to his world while at the same time severing his contact with that world. Whether interpreting Jerry as psychopath, Christ-figure, or shaman,[13] critics generally acknowledge Albee's chief thematic point regarding the play's climax: to present a Peter who, through "the cleansing consciousness of death,"[14] progresses from ignorance to awareness through Jerry's self-sacrifice. His howl—"OH MY GOD!" (49)—transcends all of his previously banal responses. Markedly altered by internalizing the force of death,

Peter will never return to routine habits, what Samuel Beckett, who greatly influenced the young Albee, calls "the great deadener" within human experience.[15] The prescribed formulas and labels around which Peter once forged his safe, middle-of-the road personal politic, Albee implies, will no longer work. Peter, like his adversary, is suddenly on "the precipice."[16] The ending of *The Zoo Story*, despite its ambiguity, suggests that Peter's subsequent language and action will be founded within a more expansive humanistic context, one in which Jerry's "teaching emotion" will forever temper his every gesture. In discussing the necessity of the stabbing Albee suggests that death is the only way Jerry can break through the well-ordered world of Peter to educate him: "Had Peter understood, had he not refused to understand, then I doubt the death would have been necessary. Jerry tries all the way through the play to teach and fails. And finally makes a last effort at teaching, and I think succeeds."[17] Implicit in Albee's remarks is the muted but palpable sense of optimism which exists throughout his theater.

The Zoo Story is a life-affirming play. Subordinating pessimism to the possibility that the individual can communicate honestly with the self and the other "during the precious time of our lives,"[18] Albee presents the potential for regeneration, a

BEGINNINGS

source of optimism which underlies the overtly aggressive text and performance. Jerry discovers a degree of religious fulfillment by giving his life. Even the setting reinforces the religious overtones of the play. The backdrop of "foliage, trees, sky" (11), the presence of light and warmth, the verdant lushness and vibrant aliveness of a "sun-drenched" park (17), and above all the day of the week, the Christian sabbath, Sunday—surely these details, while not purely Edenic, complement the possibility of repose and inner peace, of resurrection and salvation. His death liberates him from an impossible present and also confirms the presence of the "teaching emotion" he had discovered earlier. Jerry's death gives way, in brief, to nothing less than Peter's rebirth, a recharging of the spirit. Albee even suggests that "Peter has become Jerry to a certain extent."[19]

The regenerative spirit of *The Zoo Story* is not limited to the actors; Albee also directs the benevolent hostility of the play toward the audience. Such a deliberate attempt to diminish the actor/audience barrier, perhaps most noticeably dramatized nearly three decades later in *The Man Who Had Three Arms*, is central to Albee's dramatic and aesthetic theories. When Jerry dies and an absolved Peter exits, Albee would like actor and audience to become one within a collective stage

UNDERSTANDING EDWARD ALBEE

experience. By successfully mixing pity, fear, and recognition within the play's closure, Albee transfers the tragic insight Peter gains to the audience. For Albee communication shatters isolation.

The Zoo Story embodies both the civic function and aesthetic richness which Albee envisions as essential to the art of drama. The play, which made its debut in the United States at an Off Broadway theater, the Provincetown Playhouse, in New York City on 14 January 1960, also energized American theater, since the later works of Arthur Miller and Tennessee Williams had not matched their earlier achievements, and American stage once again needed to be revitalized. The dialogue in *The Zoo Story* rekindled an excitement in American theater not seen since Miller and Williams and, before them, O'Neill. *The Zoo Story* was one of the first American plays to sensitize audiences to the explosiveness of Off Broadway. And while such Albee contemporaries as Kenneth H. Brown, with *The Brig*, and Jack Gelber, with *The Connection*, under the radical tutelage of Julian Beck and Judith Malina were to fade as dramatic forces, Albee grew. On a personal level the American debut of *The Zoo Story*—even before Peter and Jerry took to the stage that winter evening in 1960—must have been a fabulous inspiration to the struggling, unknown, young Albee. After all, his play was one

BEGINNINGS

half of a twin bill, the other play being *Krapp's Last Tape*, written by none other than the world's foremost modern dramatist, one to whom Albee to this day still looks up, Samuel Beckett. Further, his first play includes the major themes he was to explore in all the others. Albee's next composition, *The American Dream*, only enhanced his reputation.

The American Dream

The myth of the American Dream permeates American literary texts. Arthur Miller, for one, explained his views concerning this animating myth and the way in which objective reality, coupled with the individual's fallibility, too often subverts its alluring promise:

The American Dream is the largely unacknowledged screen in front of which all American writing plays itself out—the screen of the perfectibility of man. Whoever is writing in the United States is using the American Dream as an ironical pole of his story. Early on we all drink up certain claims to self-perfection that are absent in a large part of the world. People elsewhere tend to accept, to a far greater degree anyway, that the conditions of life are hostile to man's pretensions. The American idea is different in the sense that we think that if we could only touch it, and live by it, there's a natural order in favor of us; and that the object of a good life is to get connected with that live and abundant order. And this forms a context of irony for the kind of stories we generally tell each other. After all, the stories of most significant literary works are of one or another kind of failure. And it's a failure *in relation to* that screen, that backdrop. I think it pervades American writing, including my own. It's there in *The Crucible*, in *All My Sons*, in *After the Fall*—an aspiration to an innocence that when defeated or frustrated can turn quite murderous, and we don't know what to do with this perversity; it never seems to "fit" us.[20]

The sense of innocence implicit in the myth of the American Dream collapses in Albee's *The American Dream*. Mommy and Daddy's dismemberment of their first son is a fitting gesture of perverse defiance, the unabashed response to a satisfaction-guaranteed market and mentality. In the play Albee used the ideological and mythic "screen" of the American Dream as the "ironical pole of his story." The then thirty-two-year-old Albee directed his satiric, ironic assault not against an American work ethic, but against a culture that placed its faith in a consumerist, materialist cosmos, a point he clarified nearly three decades after writing the play:

There's nothing wrong with the notion of making your own way. What is wrong with the myth of the American Dream is that notion that this is all that

BEGINNINGS

there is to existence! The myth is merely a part of other things. Becoming wealthy is OK, I suppose, but it is not a be all to end all. People who think that the acquisition of wealth or property or material things or power; that these are the things in life; the conspicuous consumption of material things is the answer; this creates a problem. The fact that we set arbitrary and artificial goals for ourselves is a problem, not the hard work ethic *per se*.[21]

A post-Eisenhower America, its unfettered enthusiasm for wealth and security an anodyne for the horrors of the Depression and World War II, a country flaunting its recrudescence through such conspicuous material acquisitions as the high-finned Cadillacs of the late 1950s, prompted the young Albee to rethink cultural values and assumptions, and finally, in this play, to generate combative imbalances. Satiric in tone, absurdist in technique, American in cadence, *The American Dream* was Albee's attack on what he saw as American complacency. For Albee, the humorous anger was necessary. For when he wrote the play, America's post–World War II optimism had yet to be undermined by its modern versions of regicide, the Kennedys' and King's assassinations; Vietnam and Watergate, the Beatles and the revolutionary 1960s, were yet to come. The myth of the American Dream was still a talismanic force, a fanciful lie of

the mind sustained by unprecedented free enter-
prise and unlimited hopes. Optimistic national-
ism—emblematized by the "right stuff" attitude of
the space race, technological and military prowess,
an enthusiastic renewal of faith in science as truth,
a United States–dominated Olympic Games,
youth, and, above all, money—infiltrated the
American consciousness. The American Adam was
now transformed into a postlapsarian figure, his
youthful innocence tempered (and corrupted) by a
blatantly self-reliant consumerism.

Such a cultural milieu invited the ironising of
experience, as Miller suggested. But for Albee the
social climate, which greatly crippled Broadway,
gave rise in *The American Dream* to absurdist satire.
"The play is an examination of the American
Scene," Albee emphatically announces in the pref-
ace, "an attack on the substitution of artificial for
real values in our society, a condemnation of
complacency, cruelty, emasculation and vacuity; it
is a stand against the fiction that everything in this
slipping land of ours is peachy-keen" (53–54).
Albee stages his attack through language. Recep-
tive to such influential European absurdists as
Beckett, Genet, Ionesco, and Pinter, Albee experi-
mented with the absurdist technique of devaluing
language, his often illogical, cliché-ridden repartee

BEGINNINGS

signifying the characters' banality. He quickly establishes the absurdist texture of the play when Mommy discusses the color of her hat. The length, detail, and obsession with which she analyzes the hat appears ridiculous and boring, Albee's method of capturing the superficiality of her values, the way that important energy of authentic communication is wasted on trite, meaningless expression. Like Ionesco's *The Bald Soprano*, *The American Dream* continually parodies language and definition, substitutes cliché for genuine comprehension, mocks social convention and audience expectation. "A curious feature of Albee's work," writes Paolucci, "is his early experimentation (in *The American Dream* and *The Sandbox*, for instance) along the lines of Beckett and Ionesco—the defleshed abstract stage where language becomes an irritating puzzle and familiar conventions are struck down harshly, without any effort at salvaging some measure of our experience."[22]

Albee stages Mrs. Barker's entrance as a parody of etiquette and social discourse. Mrs. Barker (often referred to as "they") introduces herself only to witness Daddy's comically repetitious forgetfulness: he can never recall "what's-her-name" (87). Albee exaggerates social awkwardness moments after her entrance, first by having Daddy announce the unexpected—"Now that you're here, I don't suppose you could go away and maybe come back some other time'' (76)—and then by having Mrs. Barker make herself too much at home:

> *Mommy*: . . . Are you sure you're comfortable? Won't you take off your dress?
> *Mrs. Barker*: I don't mind if I do. (*She removes her dress*).
> *Mommy*: There. You must feel a great deal more comfortable.
> *Mrs. Barker*: Well, I certainly *look* a great deal more comfortable.
> *Daddy*: I'm going to blush and giggle.
> *Mommy*: Daddy's going to blush and giggle.
> *Mrs. Barker* (*Pulling the hem of her slip above her knees*): You're lucky to have such a man for a husband.
> *Mommy*: Oh, don't I know it!
> *Daddy*: I just blushed and giggled and went sticky wet (79).

Throughout *The American Dream*, Albee employs this kind of dialogue, the overstated or unexpected outbursts underscoring the pettiness of the characters' lives, the smallness of vision, the ludicrousness of a world filled with empty platitudes. The overall image is one of social and spiritual entropy. Individuals are reduced to caricatures. Mommy and Daddy's directing force in life is monetary satisfaction, a goal attainable because of their belief

BEGINNINGS

in the myth of the American Dream. Their innocence long ago corrupted, however, Mommy and
Daddy again at the play's close place their faith in
a consumerist America which can deliver happiness and fulfillment through Mrs. Barker, the Bye-
Bye Adoption Service agent who delivered their
first son two decades earlier. That Mommy and
Daddy respond exactly the same way to Mrs.
Barker twenty years later highlights the stasis of
their world, the lack of any intellectual or moral
growth.

In his exposure of the American scene Albee
concentrates on Mommy and Daddy's relationship. The power of love which Jerry tried to understand in *The Zoo Story* vanishes in this play.
Love never enters in Mommy and Daddy's
nonmarriage. At first they reduced love to the
merely physical: "I have a right to live off of you
because I married you, and because I used to let
you get on top of me and bump your uglies" (67).
Presently even sexual intercourse seems beyond
possibility, Daddy's impotence—"Daddy has
tubes now, where he used to have tracts" (90)—
objectifying the physical separation of man and
woman. But their physical separateness is simply
emblematic of their spiritual aridity, which, perhaps because he too was an adopted child, the
young Albee saw as an ubiquitous condition in

American culture. Most discernible by its absence, love collapses under the pressure of Mommy's domination and Daddy's acquiescence, with hatred and indifference filling the vacant spaces. Like Mommy in *The Sandbox*, Mommy is the badgering, manipulative female, the controller and castrator of a defenseless and emasculated Daddy. And Daddy is one of several Albee male characters who earn Mommy's wrath, in part because his primary social and personal strategy is one of withdrawal, nonengagement, his path-of-least-resistance attitude leading toward isolation and an ossified spirit. Robert Martin Adams, speculating on our cultural preoccupation with Nothingness, observes that accepting Nothing "is a willful submission of oneself to non-experience as an active form of experience."[23] Daddy embraces precisely such a sense of Nothing by leading a death-in-life existence: he just wants "to get everything over with" (70). In *The American Dream*, Albee introduces no great upsetter of delicate balances, one who could dispel the corrosive influence of Nothing. Rather, he exposes the inertia paralyzing this family. This is Albee's staging of the negative epiphany, the absurdist apprehension of human intercourse, what Susan Sontag deems "the prototypically modern revelation: a negative epiphany."[24]

Grandma is the one source of vitality in the

play. Alive, articulate, Grandma neither participates in nor is entrapped by the absurdism of the dialogue. Her observations are accurate, free from the banalities of the others. Dignified though treated with disrespect, clear-sighted though elderly, Grandma represents for the author the singular source of caring, an admittedly sentimental character based on Albee's grandmother, one harkening back to an era supposedly closer to innocence. She neither acquiesces to ridicule nor makes excuses for herself. She understands and accepts her condition, her eighty-six years of experience creating an adaptability in the midst of verbal indignities. An individual living "in the age of deformity" (86), Grandma, as Ruby Cohn suggests, "represents the vigorous old frontier spirit. Grandma resembles Jerry in her independence, but age has made her crafty, and she has learned to roll with the punches."[25]

Peter in *The Zoo Story* refused to recognize certain unpleasant but real aspects of the human condition; Mommy and Daddy, living in a self-created world of diminished possibilities, are so absorbed with material "satisfaction" and external façades that even the slightest awareness of public responsibility appears to be beyond their ken. But Grandma is unique in her capacity to remain apart from the deadening conformity which renders the others deflated types; she is a saving remnant from the past who accepts an objective reality that surely would be a source of dissatisfaction to her relatives:

My sacks are empty, the fluid in my eyeballs is all caked on the inside edges, my spine is made of sugar candy, I breathe ice; but you don't hear me complain. Nobody hears old people complain because people think that's all old people do. And *that's* because old people are gnarled and sagged and twisted into the shape of a complaint (*Signs off*) (82–83).

Albee counterbalances Grandma's acceptance of the self and humanity with Mommy and Daddy's rejection of their first child. After buying the baby twenty years ago through Mrs. Barker's agency, Mommy and Daddy watched in disbelief as their boy failed to grow into their own version of the American Dream. Albee intensifies the absurdist dialogue by juxtaposing the appalling account of the dismemberment of their child with Grandma's matter-of-fact recollection:

Grandma: But that was only the beginning. Then it turned out it only had eyes for its Daddy.
Mrs. Barker: For its Daddy! Why, any self-respecting woman would have gouged those eyes right out of its head.
Grandma: Well, she did. That's exactly what she did. [. . .] But *then*, it began to develop an interest in its you-know-what.

BEGINNINGS

Mrs. Barker: In its you-know-what! Well! I hope they cut its hand off at the wrists!
Grandma: Well, yes, they did that eventually. But first, they cut off its you-know-what.
Mrs. Barker: A much better idea!
Grandma: That's what they thought. But after they cut off its you-know-what, it *still* put its hands under the covers, *looking* for its you-know-what. So, finally, they *had* to cut off its hands at the wrists.
Mrs. Barker: Naturally!
Grandma: And it was such a resentful bumble. Why, one day it called its Mommy a dirty name.
Mrs. Barker: Well, I hope they cut its tongue out!
Grandma: Of course. And then, as it got bigger, they found out all sorts of terrible things about it, like: it didn't have a head on its shoulders, it had no guts, it was spineless, its feet were made of clay . . . just dreadful things (99–101).

The child did not produce satisfaction, refused to conform, so within the inverted logic of an absurdist act Mommy and Daddy mutilated the boy. Albee further calls into question the myth of the American Dream when he suggests that Mommy and Daddy's motivation for the physical and spiritual dismemberment stems from their measurement of humanity and fulfillment completely in financial terms. As Grandma reports:

Well, for the last straw, it finally up and died; and

you can imagine how *that* made them feel, their having paid for it, and all. So, they called up the lady who sold them the bumble in the first place and told her to come right over to their apartment. They wanted satisfaction; they wanted their money back. That's what they wanted (101).

The appearance of the Young Man allows Mommy and Daddy the chance to reinvent their American Dream myth. As she did twenty years earlier, Mrs. Barker delivers the new version of a "bumble," a handsome walking symbol epitomizing the emptiness of Mommy and Daddy's values. Like his new parents he is nameless. Their namelessness is Albee's technique for diminishing their humanity; each is a human reduced to a functional type. A vain incarnation of a sterile culture, the young man admits he will "do almost anything for money" (109). He is a representative of what Martin Esslin in *The Theatre of the Absurd* calls "the corn–fed cheeriness of advertising jingles,"[26] a point the Young Man reinforces: "[I am] almost insultingly good-looking in a typically American way. Good profile, straight nose, honest eyes, wonderful smile" (107).

Curiously, the Young Man possesses some of Grandma's self-awareness, a quality that becomes evident during his reminiscence of his twin brother, a reflective moment in which he discusses

BEGINNINGS

a favorite Albee theme—a sense of loss, a "fall from grace," an inability to love: "I no longer have the capacity to feel anything. I have no emotions. I have been drained, torn asunder . . . disemboweled. . . . I am incomplete . . . I can feel nothing" (115). His account, of course, would serve as a perfect description of Mommy and Daddy, although they are incapable of such self-examination. Unlike Mommy and Daddy's first child, their second will survive because he is an actor, the perfectly pliable man, one able to don any social mask precisely because he is drained of all substance and individuality. His external attractiveness and internal spinelessness make him a suitable match for the unreal demands of Mommy and Daddy. As the satiric embodiment of the American Dream he becomes for the audience "the existential question made flesh."[27] In other words, he is the one who forces the audience to reassess what this particular family might nurture. Of course, on one level the Young Man succeeds: he brings Mommy and Daddy their most tangible form of fulfillment, material satisfaction. But the quickness with which he turns from self-awareness to mindlessness confirms the overwhelming lure of surface illusions. The last opportunity for spiritual regeneration is lost when Grandma leaves and the Young Man moves in.[28] The somewhat curious portrait of the Young Man points to Albee's keen awareness of ambivalences. The playwright is drawn to the kind of lament the Young Man voices regarding the loss of love, his fall from grace; at the same time Albee rejects those very cultural and personal attitudes which produce such defleshed persons as the Young Man and which produce spiritual dislocations, personal vacuity, and self-annihilating myths.

Much of the play's anger is directed toward the American family; from a biographical perspective perhaps Albee's own childhood accounts for part of the unsparing satire. Albee apparently viewed his mother as a domineering figure (physically she was nearly a foot taller than her husband; psychologically she seems to have developed a hostile attitude toward her family). According to the few sources available regarding Albee's childhood (even today Albee's past is off limits in interviews), his mother was the wife who tormented her weak, emasculated husband. The parents' millionaire status allowed them, it also appears, to substitute material pleasure for love. Perhaps these factors account for the anger of *The American Dream*. Such issues as rejection, abandonment, loss of love, misplaced values, and withdrawals from human commitment dominate the early plays. Perhaps Albee's homosexuality only added to the strained relations between uncaring parents and child and, in the plays, expresses itself through the intense animosity between the sexes. But Albee did genuinely love one family member— his grandmother. She shared her love, an authentic care for the young Albee; the boy in turn regarded her as the one person in the family not corrupted by wealth, the one who represented a past whose values were not tainted. "I could communicate with her," Albee recalled. "She was at the end of it and I was at the beginning. So both of us were outside the ring."[29] His feelings for Grandma Cotta explains his positive treatment of Grandma in both *The Sandbox* and *The American Dream*.

Admittedly *The American Dream* seems somewhat dated today. Audiences are now accustomed to the outrageousness of absurdist images and techniques; the political and aesthetic richness of absurdism, while still compelling, has been so incorporated into public art and mass media that its shock value has dissipated somewhat. Historically, however, the play exerted a tremendous influence on American theater following its 24 January 1961 premiere at the York Playhouse in New York City, giving inspiration and added significance to Off Broadway. *Not* an absurdist playwright, Albee nevertheless succeeded in using absurdist techniques in a play Esslin identified as a "promising and brilliant first example of an American contribution to the Theatre of the Absurd."[30] The play was also an important work dramaturgically for a still-maturing playwright struggling to forge craft into art.

As social protest theater *The American Dream* reflects "back at us the hypocrisy of much of modern American life."[31] Relationships are subordinated to social categories, and often these categories are used as psychological screens behind which the characters lose all sense of original thought or ethical purpose. The characters become mere extensions of the play's set design: they are objects, types living in a sterile apartment filled with gaudy furniture, a home which Jordan Y. Miller labels accurately as "a modern prefabricated chamber of horrors."[32] But the ultimate force of the play lies not so much in its social critique as in its existentialist presentation of the enervated individual. If the characters in the play appear beyond redemption—and there is no epiphanic moment, no coming to consciousness that might pave the way for even the possibility of salvation—it is because Albee would like to alter the audience's perceptions about the self, the other, and the cultural milieu. *The American Dream* succeeds in presenting its universal theme, "a personal, private yowl" that "has something to do with the anguish of us all" (54). Albee continued in his next play, *Who's Afraid of Virginia Woolf?* to explore the personal experience that precipitates a fundamental anguish within us, but with a success that surely exceeded his dramatic expectations.

Notes

1. Alan Prince, "An Interview with John Barth," *Prism* (1968): 62.

2. Rose A. Zimbardo, "Symbolism and Naturalism in Edward Albee's *The Zoo Story*," *Edward Albee* ed. C. W. E. Bigsby (Englewood Cliffs, NJ: Prentice-Hall, 1975) 46.

3. Leo Tolstoy, *The Death of Ivan Ilych and Other Stories* (New York: Signet, 1960) 104.

4. Anne Paolucci, *From Tension to Tonic: The Plays of Edward Albee* (Carbondale: Southern Illinois University Press, 1972) 40.

5. C. W. E. Bigsby, *A Critical Introduction to Twentieth-Century American Drama* (New York: Cambridge University Press, 1984) 2:257.

6. Edward Albee, *The Zoo Story and The American Dream* (New York: Signet, 1960) 11. The page references within the text are to this edition.

7. Matthew C. Roudané, "A Playwright Speaks: An Interview with Edward Albee," *Critical Essays on Edward Albee*, ed. Philip C. Kolin and J. Madison Davis (Boston: Hall, 1986) 199.

8. Bigsby, 258.

9. Matthew C. Roudané, "An Interview with Edward Albee," *Southern Humanities Review* 16 (1982): 38.

10. Shelly Fisher Fishkin, *From Fact to Fiction: Journalism and*

UNDERSTANDING EDWARD ALBEE

Imaginative Writing in America (Baltimore: Johns Hopkins University Press, 1985) 216.

11. Brian C. Way, "Albee and the Absurd: *The American Dream* and *The Zoo Story*," Bigsby 38.

12. Albert Camus, *The Myth of Sisyphus and Other Essays* (New York: Vintage, 1955) 10.

13. See Mary Castiglie Anderson, "Ritual and Initiation in *The Zoo Story*," *Edward Albee: An Interview and Essays*, ed. Julian N. Wasserman ed., Lee Lecture Series: University of St. Thomas, Houston, TX. (Syracuse: Syracuse University Press, 1983) 93–108.

14. Edward Albee, *The Plays* (New York: Coward, McCann, and Geohegan, 1981) 1:10.

15. Samuel Beckett, *Waiting for Godot* (New York: Grove, 1954) 58.

16. Matthew C. Roudané, "Albee on Albee," *RE: Artes Liberales* 10 (1984): 4.

17. Michael E. Rutenberg, *Edward Albee: Playwright in Protest* (New York: Avon, 1969) 220.

18. Roudané, "A Playwright Speaks" 197.

19. Roudané, "Interview with Edward Albee" 43.

20. Matthew C. Roudané, "An Interview with Arthur Miller," *Michigan Quarterly Review* 24 (1985): 374–75.

21. Roudané, "A Playwright Speaks" 195–96.

22. Anne Paolucci, "Albee and the Restructuring of the Modern Stage," *Studies in American Dream, 1945–Present* 1 (1986): 14–15.

23. Robert Martin Adams, *NIL: Episodes in the Literary Conquest of Void During the Nineteenth Century* (New York: Oxford University Press, 1966) 3.

24. Susan Sontag, *On Photography* (New York: Farrar, Straus, 1977) 19.

25. Ruby Cohn, *Edward Albee* (Minneapolis: University of Minnesota Press, 1969) 11.

26. Martin Esslin, *The Theatre of the Absurd*, rev. ed. (Woodstock, NY: Overlook Press, 1969) 268.

27. Anne Paolucci, *From Tension to Tonic: The Plays of Edward Albee* (Carbondale: Southern Illinois University Press, 1972) 34.

BEGINNINGS

28. Some critics find Albee's treatment of the Young Man ambiguous and questionable. See, for instance, Cohn 14 and Kenneth Hamilton, "Mr. Albee's Dream," *Queens Quarterly* 70 (1963): 393, 399. Critics also disagree over the symbolic value of Grandma's boxes. For Cohn they represents a coffin; for Paolucci, "the emptiness around which we wrap our illusions" (35). But it might not be too fanciful to suggest that the boxes are one of the few places in this setting where a sense of reality and acceptance are stored.

29. "Albee Odd Man in On Broadway," *Newsweek* 4 Feb. 1963: 51.

30. Esslin 268.

31. Rutenberg 74.

32. Jordan Y. Miller, "The Myth and the American Dream: O'Neill to Albee," *Modern Drama* 7 (1964): 195.

CHAPTER THREE

Toward the Marrow: *Who's Afraid of Virginia Woolf?*

Before they slept, they must fight; after they had fought, they would embrace. From that embrace, another life might be born. But first they must fight, as the dog fights with the vixen, in the heart of darkness, in fields of night.

Virginia Woolf, *Between the Acts*

Albee's status as a major dramatist, even after the excitement and notoriety of *The Zoo Story* (1959) and *The American Dream* (1961), seemed questionable. *The Sandbox, Fam and Yam,* and *The Death of Bessie Smith,* all produced in 1960, are important works insofar as revealing Albee's emerging unity of vision and skill as an inventor of acerbic dialogue, but hardly major plays. They bear the growing pains of a new playwright sorting through autobiographical, ideological, and technical concerns. Very much a product of Off Broadway, Albee was viewed by many critics as a promising but untested writer. Was he yet another American dramatist with but one or two good plays in his repertoire? Were those who praised Albee, perhaps in their eagerness to anoint the Next American Playwright, too hasty in their accolades? The night Albee stormed Broadway, 13 October 1962 at the Billy Rose Theatre in New York City, changed such suspicions. *Who's Afraid of Virginia Woolf?* unquestionably certified Albee's place in American literature. It was a play that went on to dominate the theater world in the 1960s. Finally, it seemed, a qualitatively unique voice emerged to help Tennessee Williams and Arthur Miller sustain the modern American dramatic heritage established by Eugene O'Neill. Albee's first full-length play is now ranked with some of the classics of American theater: O'Neill's *Long Day's Journey into Night*, Williams's *A Streetcar Named Desire*, and Miller's *Death of a Salesman*.

Realism and theatricalism—a fusion of the illusion of reality and dramaturgic invention—coalesce in *Who's Afraid of Virginia Woolf?* More specifically, its relentless verbal dueling, Strindbergian sexual tension, and unexpected exorcism within a claustrophobic set generated tremendous excitement and outrage, as Gilbert Debusscher points out:

The quarrel over *The American Dream* had scarcely died down when Albee exploded a veritable bomb. *Who's*

Afraid of Virginia Woolf? immediately became the subject of the most impassioned controversies, the object of criticism and accusation which recall the storms over the first plays of Ibsen and, closer to our own time, Beckett and Pinter. If we are able to examine this play today with more serenity, we are nonetheless forced to acknowledge its content might well have outraged the orthodox public of Broadway.[1]

Although not without its stylistic flaws the play was attacked by many for its destructive theme. For instance, Harold Clurman, acknowledging Albee's "superbly virile and pliant" dialogue, nonetheless concludes that "the pessimism and rage of *Who's Afraid of Virginia Woolf?* are immature";[2] Diana Trilling distorts Albee's intent, arguing that "the 'message' of Mr. Albee's play couldn't be more terrible: life is nothing, and we must have the courage to face our emptiness without fear";[3] and Richard Schechner implies that the play celebrates decadent values, embracing "self-pity, drooling, womb-seeking weakness, . . . the persistent escape into morbid fantasy."[4] These assessments typified an astonishing number of the early reactions to the play, culminating in certain members of the Pulitzer Prize committee refusing to bestow the award it so clearly earned because, as one member of the committee claimed, it was "a

TOWARD THE MARROW

filthy play."[5] In turn, other members who supported Albee's nomination resigned from the committee in protest.

Even today many scholars fail to recognize the unmistakably affirmative nature of the play.[6] One of the most compelling features of the play's ending is the resilience of George and Martha's collective imagination to reinvent reality by subordinating illusion to truth, a profound recognition of the regenerative powers implicit in facing human existence without what Henrik Ibsen in *The Wild Duck* termed "life-lies." Albee himself often alludes to the affirmative texture of his masterpiece. As he points out, the play challenges the sorts of illusions paralyzing the figures in O'Neill's *The Iceman Cometh*, one of the plays that motivated Albee to present George and Martha's condition. "It's about going against the 'pipe dreams.' After all, *Who's Afraid of Virginia Woolf?* just says have your pipe dreams if you want to but realize you are kidding yourself."[7]

The play's three-act structure chronicles George and Martha's realization that their pipe dream—their imaginary son—is kidding as well as killing them. But such recognition comes only after twenty-one years of fabricating and nurturing their child-illusion. Private mythology turns to public issue, however, early in act 1 when Martha's offstage remarks to Honey about their son signals an ominous shift in her marriage relationship and in the psychodynamics of the games the characters play. Albee establishes the importance of Martha's revelation not only through dialogue, but through George's nonverbal response:

> Honey (*To George, brightly*): I didn't know until just a minute ago that you had a *son*.
> George (*Wheeling, as if struck from behind*): WHAT?[8]

Albee creates a sense of mystery regarding their son; George and Martha will continually allude to their child, but always with a felt tension, a "nervous friction"[9] between them. Not until the exorcism will the audience, with Nick and Honey, realize that the son is a fiction. The intensity of George's question to Honey suggests the seriousness of Martha's slip, a violation of their lifelong agreement never publicly to "start in on the bit about the kid" (18). That Honey, an outsider, suddenly possesses knowledge of their son certifies the enormity of their illusion. What originally started out as mere game playing, the lovers' fanciful procreation of a symbolic child they could never have, has grown into the bizarre "representation of a warped, sadomasochistic relationship."[10] By breaking the unwritten laws of the

TOWARD THE MARROW

game Martha unwittingly forces a definitive confrontation regarding their grasp on objective reality. More than a social embarrassment—after all,
what's so unusual about mentioning one's child?—
Martha's publicizing their son's existence signals,
George recognizes, that their private life has disin-
tegrated into an unreal, terrifying make-believe
world. Distinctions between truth and illusion become blurred, not by the continual drinking but
because of a psychotic reliance on fiction as truth.
George's refrain—"Truth and illusion. Who knows
the difference, eh, toots? Eh?" (201)—becomes a
disarming refrain, a haunting monody throughout
the play. But this refrain also testifies to George's
awareness of and commitment to sorting through
the real and the imaginary, and places his cruel
verbal attacks in a broader context. George confirms the point when the comic outburst defers to
the tragic insight:

But you've taken a new tack, Martha, over the past
couple of centuries—or however long it's been I've
lived in this house with you—that makes it just too
much . . . too much. I don't mind your dirty under-
things in public . . . well, I *do* mind, but I've recon-
ciled myself to that . . . but you've moved bag and
baggage into your own fantasy world now, and
you've started playing variations on your own distortions, and, as a result . . . (155).

His lines taper off, but Albee's suggestion is clear: Martha, and perhaps George, will lose sight of objective reality if they do not banish their distortions.

From early in act 1 onward, most of George's social and psychological strategies center on one goal: to exorcise the son-illusion perverting their lives. Within this context, then, George and Martha's brutalizing language, which escalates with each act, becomes a necessary social and psychological dynamic. In other words, the final expiation of the illusion is made possible by externalizing the lies governing their, and Nick and Honey's, relationship through such games as "Hump the Hostess," "Get the Guests," and finally "Bringing Up Baby." Conflict precedes resolution.

Although *Who's Afraid of Virginia Woolf?* stages a "war between the sexes,"[11] Albee's ultimate interest lies in presenting love as a unifying presence. He supplants the lack of compassion in *The Death of Bessie Smith* and the apathy in *The American Dream* with George and Martha's reciprocal care and love. Love's opposite—indifference—finds no place in their marriage. Albee's dialogue mixes kindness and cruelty, Jerry's "teaching emotion," making George and Martha's verbal clashes, for better or worse, an ineluctable element of their relationship. Thus George can accurately describe his wife as a "spoiled, self-indulgent, willful, dirty-minded, liquor-ridden" woman (157), and Martha with equal accuracy can counter with verbal salvos, as when she attacks his professional shortcomings:

You see, George didn't have much . . . push . . . he wasn't particularly . . . aggressive. In fact he was sort of a . . . (*Spits the word at George's back*) . . . A FLOP! A great . . . big . . . fat . . . FLOP! (84).

They are, Albee observes, "equal competitors."[12] But their wittily devastating repartee is born out of a profound love for the other, a point they lose sight of but regain in act 3.

Hate precedes the restoration of love, however. Martha's vicious attacks cast her, as a "domineering wife, another 'braying,' bossy bitch," a fully developed Mommy figure.[13] Although her tirades plainly exceed the limits of expected social devoir, Martha's actions at least become more understandable in light of her past. Like Jerry in *The Zoo Story* and Grandma in *The Sandbox*, Martha feels abandoned, and with some justification. Her mother's death left her to be raised by her father, a man she "absolutely worshipped" (77). But she grows up with a father who "doesn't give a damn whether she lives or dies, who couldn't care less *what* happens to his only daughter" (225). Psychologically abandoned, she seeks to reinvent a loving home through her marriage to George, who at the time fulfilled her romantic desires: "And along came George. That's right. WHO was young . . . intelligent . . . and . . . bushy-tailed, and . . . sort of cute . . . if you can imagine it" (81). But reality subverts her romantic heroic ideal during the course of a twenty-year marriage, her present warring nature prompted by years of frustrated ambitions and diminished hopes.

Of course, Martha does little to better her predicament. Victimized by her own sense of loss, she vents her fury, like Jo in *The Lady from Dubuque*, on those around her. "Without any sense of how she can contribute to improve the quality of her life," Anita Maria Stenz explains, "expecting all things great and beautiful to come from outside herself, she wallows in disillusionment. With nothing to do that interests her and nothing to live for, she spends her night leaving a trail of half-filled glasses of gin around the house and her days sleeping off her drunkenness."[14] And her husband exacerbates her sense of loss.

George contributes to their troubled condition by withdrawing from confrontation and commitment. He has drifted from the "total engagement" that the Mistress in *All Over* knows must be present if a relationship is to be meaningful.[15] Professionally as well as personally he compromises his being, inviting Martha's wrath: he was "expected to *be* somebody, not just some nobody, some bookworm, somebody who's so damn . . . contemplative, he can't make anything out of himself, somebody without the *guts* to make anybody proud of him . . ." (85). George's social strategy of withdrawal, Albee suggests, expands into a nearly death-in-life pattern, his intellectual screens blocking him from attending to the self and the other authentically. Anesthetizing routines preempt honest engagement, as George admits:

I'm numbed enough . . . and I don't mean by liquor, though maybe that's been part of the process—a gradual, over-the-years going to sleep of the brain cells— I'm numbed enough, now, to be able to take you when we're alone. I don't listen to you . . . or when I *do* listen to you, I sift everything, I bring everything down to reflex response, so I don't really *hear* you, which is the only way to manage it (155).

Albee also raises questions about George's adolescent rite of passage—earning a driver's license—and the way in which the pastness of the past psychologically affects his present condition. Albee carefully works with the Bergin story, the tale in which George's high school acquaintance, learning to drive, swerved to miss an animal, demolishing the car against a tree and killing his father. George wraps up the story for Nick:

> He was not killed, of course. And in the hospital, when he was conscious and out of danger, and when they told him that his father *was* dead, he began to laugh, I have been told, and his laughter grew and he would not stop, and it was not until after they jammed a needle in his arm, not until after that, until his consciousness slipped away from him, that his laughter subsided . . . stopped. And when he was recovered from his injuries enough so that he could be moved without damage should he struggle, he was put in an asylum. That was thirty years ago.
> *Nick*: Is he . . . still there?
> *George*: Oh, yes. And I'm told that for these thirty years he has . . . not . . . uttered . . . one . . . sound (96).

Ambiguous and mysterious, the story within a play complements the broader truth/illusion motif of the drama. Albee keeps the audience off balance, for the theatergoer never knows if George is a "stage magician" or not. Is he fabricating, as Williams poeticizes in *The Glass Menagerie*, an "illusion that has the appearance of truth" or a "truth in the pleasant disguise of illusion"?[16] The ambiguity and mystery of the Bergin story increase with

TOWARD THE MARROW

Martha's disclosure of George's past, a past mimicking the tragic events of the tale and reexperienced in his unpublished nonfiction novel. If the audience believes Martha, and the evidence supports her claims, the boy in the Bergin story is a persona for George. In other words, George killed his father in exactly the same way the boy did. Albee strengthens the correspondence between George's fictive and actual experiences by elevating emotional intensity, the verbal duel turning, for the first time during the evening, to the physical assault:

Martha: Georgie said [to Martha's father] . . . but Daddy . . . I mean . . . ha, ha, ha, ha . . . but *Sir*, it isn't a *novel* at all . . . (*Other voice*) Not a novel? (*Mimicking George's voice*) No, sir . . . it isn't a novel at all . . .
George (*Advancing on her*): You will not say this!
Nick (*Sensing the danger*): Hey.
Martha: The hell I won't. Keep away from me, you bastard! (*Backs off a little . . . uses George's voice again*) No, Sir, this isn't a novel at all . . . this is the truth . . . this really happened . . . TO ME!
George (*On her*): I'LL KILL YOU! (*Grabs her by the throat. They struggle*)
Nick: HEY! (*Comes between them*)
Honey (*Wildly*): VIOLENCE! VIOLENCE! (*George, Martha, and Nick struggle . . . yells, etc.*)
Martha: IT HAPPENED! TO ME! TO ME!

George: YOU SATANIC BITCH!
Nick: STOP THAT! STOP THAT!
Honey: VIOLENCE! VIOLENCE! (*The other three struggle. George's hands are on Martha's throat. Nick grabs him, tears him from Martha, throws him on the floor. George, on the floor; Nick over him; Martha to one side, her hand on her throat*)
Nick: That's enough now! (136–38).

On a thematic level the Bergin story and George's violent reaction to it suggest that he is as vulnerable, anguished, and confused as Martha. Except for such outbursts he simply hides his condition better. Like Martha he has immersed himself in fantasy. Their individual fantasy worlds dovetail, of course, with the child-illusion.

Unlike Martha, however, George possesses a compelling integrity, a belief in certain humanistic moral principles. Although he has not distinguished himself as a historian and withdraws into his own self, George earns the audience's sympathy and admiration—sympathy because of an ability to withstand the emotional hazing, admiration because of an ability to restore a qualitative order, based on love, to their marriage by the final curtain. One of his most significant insights is understanding that they have *both* "moved bag and baggage" (155) into a psychotic make-believe world; that *both* suffer from a collective inability to

TOWARD THE MARROW

accept truth over illusion; and that their games have descended into a form of madness. But the chief difference between the two concerns objectivity: he alone detaches himself from the illusion, thereby enabling him to help Martha restore psychic balance. At times even Martha, in lines demonstrating her love for George, pinpoints the issue:

. . . George who is out somewhere there in the dark
. . . George who is good to me, and whom I revile;
who understands me, and whom I push off; who can
make me laugh, and I choke it back in my throat; who
can hold me, at night, so that it's warm, and whom I
will bite so there's blood; who keeps learning the
games we play as quickly as I can change the rules;
who can make me happy and I do not wish to be
happy, and yes I do wish to be happy. George and
Martha: sad, sad, sad (190–91).

Armed with such an ability to absorb changes in the rules of the game, George sets his sights on banishing from their existence their greatest failure and most debilitating illusion.

Nick and Honey find themselves caught in the crossfire. Further, they become active participants in the war. Opportunistic and smug, handsome and intelligent, Nick seems mostly interested in "plow[ing] a few pertinent wives" (112) at the college. Honey accepts her husband's patronizing and falsely solicitous gestures, and appears least equipped to deal with the evening's strangeness. Honey is a woman "who blushes over any mention of sex and has about as much substance as cotton candy."[17] Together, Nick and Honey form a well-meaning but weak couple.

Their contributions to the play, however, allow the audience to view Nick as more than an emotional punching bag and Honey a comedic doll. In certain important respects, as one critic argues, the younger couple's relationship mirrors George and Martha's.[18] The most conspicuous parallels concern the childlessness and the nonmarriages of the two couples. Honey fabricates her own story, her false pregnancy, a diversionary tactic, a method of avoiding her reality—her terror of having children. Her inability to communicate her predicament to Nick, who probably doesn't want to hear much about harsh truths, leads to a marriage predicated more on social appearances than on love. Honey appears happy as long as her illusions remain intact. And her strategy plays directly into Nick's role as the dominant partner within their relationship. But her outburst testifies to the intensity of a deep-rooted anxiety with which, to this point, neither she nor Nick has come to terms:

NO! . . . I DON'T WANT ANY . . . I DON'T WANT

TOWARD THE MARROW

THEM. . . . GO 'WAY. . . . (*Begins to cry*) I DON'T
WANT . . . ANY . . . CHILDREN. . . . I . . . don't
. . . want . . . any . . . children. I'm afraid! I don't
want to be hurt. . . . PLEASE! (176).

By admitting to her existentialist fear, Honey paves
the way for the possibility of an authentic life with
herself and those within her orbit, a possibility
manifest in her announcement near the play's end,
"I want a child. I want a baby" (223). Her words
have a cathartic influence, signaling a first step in
facing reality without the encumbrances of illusions. Honey, Albee suggests, will also force Nick
to rethink the nature of his life and marriage, just
as George and Martha's honesty at the play's end
forces them to reassess their lives.

Albee subverts the audience's expectations in
Who's Afraid of Virginia Woolf? That is, until Nick's
recognition of the son-as-fiction minutes before the
end, we assume the young man lives: all dialogue
reinforces his existence, especially the clarity with
which George and Martha recall his birth and early
years. Precisely because of their obsessive identifi-
cation with their son, who now assumes a most
real place within Martha's consciousness, George
enacts the ritualistic exorcism. To orchestrate the
exorcism, he first must discover "some way to
really get at" Martha (156), to enrage her inner
demons already released in *Walpurgisnacht* to a

psychological breaking point; hence the escalation to "total war" (159).

George arranges fiction to reorder reality. Confiding to Honey news that his "son . . . is . . . DEAD!" (180), George begins the exorcising process. He discusses the need to "peel labels" (212), a reference to stripping away emotional attachments blocking Martha from accepting the death of their son. While he seems unsure of his exact procedure, George knows how far the peeling process must go:

> We all peel labels, sweetie; and when you get through the skin, all three layers, through the muscle, slosh aside the organs (*An aside to Nick*) them which is still sloshable—(*Back to Honey*) and get down to bone . . . you know what you do then?
> *Honey* (*Terribly interested*): No!
> *George*: When you get down to bone, you haven't got all the way, yet. There's something inside the bone . . . the marrow . . . and that's what you gotta get at. (*A strange smile at Martha*) (212–13).

Symbolically, as George probes from the skin toward the marrow, so, Albee suggests, the aware individual must explore the various levels of consciousness, from the surface to the deeper levels of perception and experience.

Albee creates the image of George as surgeon. Like the surgeon George carefully probes into the

TOWARD THE MARROW

metaphysical body of his patient, Martha. As the doctor relies on assistants, so George uses assistants, Nick and Honey, whose participation in the ritual makes for a successful operation. It is an ontological operation. And the directing force for the metaphysical procedure is involvement: to "get at" the marrow means to demythologize the child, to excise the incubi haunting their psyches, to restore, finally, spiritual health. Although the prognosis for full recovery remains tenuous at best, George takes responsibility for the process.

Playing the game by his rules, George guides Martha through the ritual, providing the objective corrective when needed, the loving assurance when necessary. The dramatic focus is on the depth and power of Martha's psychic attachment to their myth, a child whose existence for twenty-one years counterbalanced the barrenness of their marriage, whose presence was created out of a "fear" (219) of unfulfillment, an existentialist experience of Nothingness.

George evolves from metaphysical surgeon to high priest exorcist. When Martha becomes transfixed on her child, and hurts the most, spreading her hands in a crucifixion pose, George recites the Mass of the Dead. Through these hypnotic scenes Albee places the viewer or reader within "the marrow" of the play. Her illusion shattered by her son's car accident (the third and final presentation of the Bergin story), Martha cleanses her soul—"(*A howl which weakens into a moan*): NOOOOOOoooooo" (233)—her purging cry signifying the death of the illusion and the rebirth of some semblance of sanity.

The denouement of the play suggests that the son-myth, for now, has vanished. A *"hint of communion"* (238) between George and Martha indicates the start of a loving armistice, a definitive change in their relationship. The play's closure, with its Joycean affirmative texture, implies more than a reconciliation of man and wife; it further implies that they can now accept their life, its cajoling ambiguity and terrifying flux included, without illusion. In their resolution they, and perhaps Nick and Honey, acknowledge the Dread implicit in human existence and affirm the importance of living honestly. The messy inconclusiveness of the play's closure, then, minimizes sentimentality while functioning thematically: Albee provides no promise that their marriage will be redeemed, that the illusion is inexorably shattered. But he does present the very real possibility for a truthful, loving renaissance for his heroes. Their new-tempered union will be measured in terms of their willingness to keep at bay the illusion that at one time was a source of happiness but, on this

TOWARD THE MARROW

night in New Carthage, erupted in all its appalling forms.

Notes

1. Gilbert Debusscher, *Edward Albee: Tradition and Renewal*, trans. Anne D. Williams (Brussels: Center for American Studies, 1967) 47.

2. Harold Clurman, *"Who's Afraid of Virginia Woolf?" Edward Albee*, ed. C. W. E. Bigsby (Englewood Cliffs, NJ: Prentice-Hall, 1975) 77, 78.

3. Diana Trilling, "The Riddle of Albee's *Who's Afraid of Virginia Woolf?"* Bigsby 85.

4. Richard Schechner, "Who's Afraid of Edward Albee?" Bigsby 63.

5. For further details see Wendal V. Harris, "Morality, Absurdity, and Albee," *Southwest Review* 29 (1964): 249–56.

6. For a detailed survey of scholarship on the play, see "Introduction," *Critical Essays on Edward Albee*, ed. Philip C. Kolin and J. Madison Davis (Boston: Hall, 1986).

7. Matthew C. Roudané, "An Interview with Edward Albee," *Southern Humanities Review* 16 (1982): 38.

8. Edward Albee, *Who's Afraid of Virginia Woolf?* (New York: Atheneum, 1962) 44. The page references within the text are to this edition.

9. Ronald Hayman, *Edward Albee* (New York: Ungar, 1971) 40.

10. Foster Hirsch, *Who's Afraid of Edward Albee?* (Berkeley: Creative Arts, 1978) 30.

11. Richard E. Amacher, *Edward Albee*, rev. ed. (Boston: Twayne, 1982) 68.

12. Roudané 39.

13. Laura Julier, "Faces to the Dawn: Female Characters in Albee's Plays," *Edward Albee: Planned Wilderness*, ed. Patricia De La Fuente, (Edinburg, TX. Pan American University Press, 1980) 35.

14. Anita Maria Stenz, *Edward Albee: The Poet of Loss* (The Hague: Mouton, 1978) 43.

15. Edward Albee, *All Over* (New York: Atheneum, 1971) 14.

16. Tennessee Williams, *The Glass Menagerie* (New York: New Directions, 1970) 22.

17. Julier 37.

18. Anne Paolucci, *From Tension to Tonic: The Plays of Edward Albee* (Carbondale: Southern Illinois University Press, 1972) 48–51.

CHAPTER FOUR

Betrayals: *Tiny Alice* and *A Delicate Balance*

Having achieved an epochal Broadway debut with *Who's Afraid of Virginia Woolf?* and after a well-received adaptation of Carson McCullers's *The Ballad of the Sad Cafe* (1963), Albee demonstrated with *Tiny Alice* a refusal to compromise artistic instinct for box office revenue, an eagerness to take aesthetic risks, a delight in challenging an orthodox Broadway sensibility. The play remains one of his more baffling productions. By now each new Albee work spawned divided loyalties, the Albeephobe's outrageous attack matched by the Albeephile's fevered defense. *Tiny Alice*, which opened 29 December 1964 at New York City's Billy Rose Theatre, only intensified the critical wars. The play was so confusing that many asked Albee to explain the "obscure points in the play" in an author's note for the published text version. "I have decided against creating such a guide," responded Albee, "because I find—after reading the play over—that I share the view of even more people: that the play is quite clear."[1]

However, in his opening remarks for a press conference Albee clearly and rather fully explained some of the mysteries of what he called "a metaphysical dream play":

Tiny Alice is a fairly simple play, and not at all unclear, once you approach it on its own terms. The story is simply this:

A lay brother, a man who would have become a priest except that he could not reconcile his idea of God with the God which men create in their own image, is sent by his superior to tie up loose ends of a business matter between the church and a wealthy woman. The lay brother becomes enmeshed in an environment which, at its core and shifting surface, contains all the elements which have confused and bothered him throughout his life: the relationship between sexual hysteria and religious ecstasy; the conflict between selflessness of service and the conspicuous splendor of martyrdom. The lay brother is brought to the point, finally, of having to accept what he had insisted he wanted, . . . union with the abstraction, rather than [a] man-made image of it, its substitution. He is left with pure abstraction—whatever it be called: God, or Alice—and in the end, according to your faith, one of two things happens: either the abstraction personifies itself, is proved real, or the dying man, in the last necessary effort of self-delusion creates and believes in what he knows does not exist.

BETRAYALS

It is, you see, a perfectly straightforward story, dealt with in terms of reality and illusion, symbol and actuality. It is the very simplicity of the play, I think, that has confused so many.[2]

Albee's remarks, while undoubtedly helpful, do not (nor should they) fully account for the events unfolding before the theatergoer.

Tiny Alice is a provocative, if not fully successful, examination of the role of truth and illusion, and the way in which truth and illusion influence the individual's religious convictions. The play concerns Julian, a lay brother who, upon his cardinal's orders, tries to finalize a multimillion-dollar donation to the church, which will be given by Miss Alice. She is beautiful—and happens to be the wealthiest woman on earth. He enters her house, a castle, only to find himself the object of a conspiracy: Lawyer, Butler, Miss Alice, even Cardinal, succeed in destroying Julian's faith in God. They convince him that he worships a denatured abstraction of God, not God himself. Julian's quest for meaning and his fear of the unknown leave him completely vulnerable to his antagonists' scheme, which culminates in Julian's marriage to Tiny Alice (not, as he thinks, to Miss Alice), yet another abstraction, a false deity who lives in the model of the castle. When Julian protests and threatens to thwart his enemies, he is shot. As he lies bleeding to death, he finally confronts an appalling reality: that he cannot rely on metaphysical abstractions; that he has been betrayed by his own faith; and that consciousness is pain.

Undoubtedly the play's obscurity and mystery, its homosexual overtones, and its apparent indictment of the church sparked the critical jousting. And the ruthlessness of the Lawyer and Butler, the seductiveness of Miss Alice, and the complicity of the Cardinal, forming an unholy assault on Julian, the lay brother, only added to Albee's reputation as a bold social protester. However, once again Albee's real interest centers not so much on public crimes of business and of church as on private crimes of the heart. He raises broader epistemic issues than in the earlier plays, as staged through Julian's various struggles: the ambiguous tensions created through truth and illusion, abstract and concrete knowledge, the relationship between sexual ecstasy and religious celebration, and, of course, man's idea of God versus the reality of God. Even the model of the castle, an exact replica of the stage set, functions to objectify the complexity and mystery of the universe in which ambivalences are the norm.

On one level Julian seems an honorable man, one whose selfless devotion to God earns the audience's admiration; he performs all tasks duti-

BETRAYALS

fully, faithfully. Serving his fellowman and God fulfills Julian, as his directing force in life evolves around self-effacing gestures: "The house of God is so grand . . . (*Sweet apologetic smile*) it needs many servants" (57). As William F. Lucey observes, Julian is an innocent, benevolent person whose "prideful ambition led him to be the most attentive, most dedicated of servants."[3] He refuses to compromise his search for God, and is unwilling to embrace false deity—even though he cannot fully certify his own faith. In certain respects Julian is,—like Jerry in *The Zoo Story* and George in *Who's Afraid of Virginia Woolf?*—a truth seeker. This is why Mary E. Campbell sees Julian as one possessing "far fewer frailties than most of us mortals. Albee has formed him with marked success, for he is able to stand up to the considerable dramatic competition of his antagonists, and is personally a thoroughly admirable kind of man, courageous and good, sensitive and scrupulous both spiritually and intellectually."[4] Hence the image of Julian the kindhearted, one victimized by an evil conspiracy, an Everyman brutalized by the business-as-sacrament world of Miss Alice and cohorts.

On another level, however, Julian appears as an immature, naïve fifty-year-old. He has withdrawn, Albee suggests, from the complex responsibilities that go with being an aware adult. Hiding

behind the mask of the ministry becomes an unconscious social stratagem, a convenient method of
evading reality, of avoiding confrontations with a
secularized world in which people worship a representative of God more often than God himself.
Sexually repressed and spiritually confused, Julian
appears as a cosmic waif, confused by his belief in
a God who is at once tangible and real, but who
also seems unfathomable unless externalized in
abstract, and therefore denatured, form. His adult
life consists of a series of tactful evasions designed
to confirm Christian mythology despite some disturbing possibilities: that such faith is verifiable
only through corrupt secular agents and abstractions; that serving humanity is meaningless; that
greed and money subvert the Cardinal and the
church; that scorn undercuts humility; that the
ultimate mysteries of the universe are better left
mysteries; and that his own blood will ultimately
"lubricate" the "great machinery" powering the
Lawyer's schemes (148). Julian's attitudes seem
conspicuous when the viewer realizes that his
words and deeds are largely cover-ups for a terribly insecure man transferring to the church all
responsibility that goes with being a mature adult.
Ironically enough, then, Julian appears "dedicated
to the reality of things, rather than their appearance" (138) but succumbs to the very symbols

BETRAYALS

which he professes to renounce. Unable to reconcile himself "... to the chasm between the nature of God and the use to which men put ... God" (44), realizing he should worship "God the creator, not the God created by man" (44), Julian retreats from living itself, using the church to absorb outside pressures and conveniently absolve him of responsibility. Thus he abrogates any individual power: "(*Quivering with intensity*) I WISH TO SERVE AND ... BE FORGOTTEN" (121).

Julian leads a death-in-life existence. Like Charlie in *Seascape*, Julian chooses the path of lesser resistance regarding social encounters, shrugging off duty in the guise of decorum. "I will not ... I will not concern myself with ... all this" (40) becomes one of his life's characteristic responses. But the Lawyer's verbal punch serves as a pitiful reminder of Julian's powerlessness: "You're quite right: bow your head, stop up your ears and do what you're told" (41). More a mannequin subjugated to evil forces than a human being fighting with a sense of purpose, Julian is the indecisive man, conscious enough to discern the importance of one's capacity to distinguish clearly between truth and illusion but confused and frightened by sexual engagement and the ontological status of God. Julian lacks the moral courage to act definitively, to sort through the experiential thicket embodied within an outer world filled with duplicity and choice. In this sense he is like the Nurse in *The Death of Bessie Smith* and anticipates what the Woman in *Listening* recalls: "We don't have to live, you know, unless we wish to; [. . .] the greatest sin in living is doing it badly—stupidly, or as if you weren't really alive."[5] This is Julian's greatest sin, a withdrawal into an unreal world, an election to sequester himself within the confines of passive nonexperience. Living as if he were not present to the external world, he becomes a doll-like figure, suitable for imprisonment in the *"doll's-house"* (23), Albee's description of the model of the castle. Innocence in Julian must be understood, then, not so much as naïveté or freedom from evil corruption but as a betrayal of the self, a collapse into unforgivable ignorance. "Innocence in a fifty year old man," Anita Marie Stenz correctly asserts, "can only be described as grotesque."[6]

Clearly Julian is no match for his adversaries. Lawyer and Butler view him as a mere object for their manipulation. They both know that Julian "is walking on the edge of an abyss" and "can be pushed . . . over, back to the asylums" or "over . . . to the Truth" (106). Moreover, Lawyer and Butler display an awareness of human frailty and doubt, a point confirmed throughout *Tiny Alice* by their self-conscious playacting in which they often

BETRAYALS

discuss man's self-fabricated "Gingerbread God with the raisin eyes" (106). Shrewd and calculating, and probably realistic, Lawyer and Butler understand that for people like Julian, God becomes real when perceived as a prop or symbol, even though such emblematic reconstruction is an inadequate formulation of Him. This is why Lawyer argues:

The mouse. Believe it. Don't personify the abstraction, Julian, limit it, demean it. Only the mouse, the toy. And that does not exist . . . but is all that can be worshipped. . . . Cut off from it, Julian, ease yourself, ease off. No trouble now; accept it (107).

Unable to impose divine order on the messiness of human desire, Julian falls from grace. Lawyer and cohorts, supreme manufacturers of sin, accept the necessity of the scar; Julian cannot. Julian resists initiation into a noncloistered world because such a reality embodies modes of experience—temptation, free will, sexual intercourse, choice—which he cannot resolve and which he has sidestepped for years. As Lawyer bluntly explains:

(*Sarcasm is gone; all is gone, save fact*) Dear Julian; we all serve, do we not? Each of us his own priesthood; publicly, some, others . . . within only; but we all do—what's-his-name's special trumpet, or clear lonely bell. Predestination, fate, the will of God, accident . . .

All swirled up in it, no matter what the name. And being man, we have invented choice, and have, indeed, gone further, and have catalogued the underpinnings of choice. But we do not know. Anything. End prologue (160).

Miss Alice appears as an evil conspirator, a sophistic temptress hastening Julian's fall. After all, she deceives and seduces the lay brother and is an accomplice to his murder. And yet she provides him with what Jerry in *The Zoo Story* calls "the teaching emotion." As she understands the mercurial nature of reality, so she accepts (and contributes to) its flaws. When Julian suggests that "we . . . simplify our life . . . as we grow older," she interjects the vital distinction: "But from understanding and acceptance; not from . . . emptying ourselves" (114–15). Within Albee's presentation Miss Alice counters Julian's habitual emptying patterns of withdrawal. He pontificates. She provides, Albee implies, a healthy dose of skepticism: "The history of the Church shows half its saints were martyrs, martyred either for the Church, or by it. The chronology is jammed with death-seekers and hysterics: the bloodbath to immortality, Julian. Joan was only one of the suicides" (121).

Her seduction of Julian is part deception, part realism, the lovemaking symbolic of his reentry

BETRAYALS

into truth, the "teaching emotion" concretized through the release of repressed sexual desires:

Oh no, my little Julian, there are no games played here; this is for keeps, and in dead earnest. There *are* cruelties, for the insulation breeds a strange kind of voyeurism; and there is impatience, too, over the need to accomplish what should not be explained; and, at the end of it, a madness of sorts . . . but a triumph (123).

Thus, on one hand Miss Alice performs her role as trickster. She deceives Julian into marrying, not herself—Miss Alice—but Alice, "the mouse in the model," the abstraction "that can be understood" (107). On the other hand she exerts a positive influence on Julian. Transforming religious celebration into sexual ecstasy through lovemaking, Julian—for the first time in years—participates in a *real* experience. Through Miss Alice he begins regenerating his spirit. Through Miss Alice he experiences the ontological difference between abstract and concrete knowledge. And after marriage Julian "is like a bubbling little boy" (140). The ambiguity of concrete truth paralyzes him. He enters into the most profound relationship of his life, only to discover that he has wedded a replica dwelling within the model of the castle, Tiny Alice.

Since the model of the castle functions as a microcosm of Miss Alice's castle and, by extension, of the outer world, Tiny Alice becomes as real as anything else within the inverted logic of the play. Miss Alice is a surrogate, an agent consummating Julian's marriage to Tiny Alice. In the midst of a kind of epistemological vertigo, Julian short-circuits his rational faculties to fit the demands of external reality: as people accept their faith in God as reality, so Julian must accept as reality his faith in Tiny Alice. The constant role playing of Lawyer, Butler, and Miss Alice reinforces the point, undermining Julian's ability to identify what is morally defensible, what seems empirically conclusive. Even the Cardinal playacts, assuring Julian that the marriage to Tiny Alice is the real thing, which he must accept on faith since, as Julian protests, "THERE IS NOTHING THERE!" (164). Pressed into the conspiracy the Cardinal stutters, "Uh . . . yes, Julian, an . . . act of faith, indeed. It is . . . believed" (165).

By act 3 Julian experiences the existentialist sense of absurdity and isolation. He rebels against the Nothingness, refuses "to be MOCKED" (166). Albee again combines kindness and cruelty as the teaching emotion, as Julian's coming to consciousness is realized through death. Victimized by the unholy tricksters, Julian finally leaves his past life of "dull waste" (33) and confronts his own being with clearer resolution. He passes from ignorance to awareness, incurring the penalty of perception: "Consciousness, then, is pain" (181). Julian now comprehends, Albee implies, Camus's philosophy—"For everything begins with consciousness and nothing is worth anything except through it"[7]—although his newfound perception is born out of the negative epiphany.

Spiritually bereft and mortally wounded, Julian internalizes the concept of nonbeing. With finality the abstraction of death turns into a concrete presence. His closest death experience, he recalls in a stream-of-consciousness outpouring, occurred when he ripped his leg open on a piece of "jagged iron" (186). Now, bleeding from the Lawyer's gunshot, there will be no grandfather to save him, no God to redeem him. "There is nothing; there is no one," he murmurs (188). With the light in the model fading and audible breathing and heartbeats filling the theater, Julian succumbs to his new secular faith. As an act of faith, a way to confirm the presence of a God, as a last pathetic gesture to believe in some divine presence, Julian accepts Tiny Alice as God: "I accept thee, Alice, for thou art come to me. God, Alice . . . I accept thy will" (190).

Tiny Alice is a dreamplay. Albee objectifies the

ethical dilemmas and contradictions within Julian's subconscious. In his search for truth Julian discovers that consciousness, in Mary Castiglie Anderson's words, "brings with it the recognition of unconscious forces and existential alienation, and that it leads ultimately to self-confrontation."[8] Albee stages the inner conflicts of Julian's psyche, dramatizing, as Thomas P. Adler suggests, "man's need for concretizing the abstract, for anthropomorphizing the Unknown."[9] Julian tries, without success, to establish his humanity by making the abstract concrete. His acceptance of Alice suggests he "believes in what he knows does not exist," as Albee explained.[10] Thematically Albee suggests that the substitution of illusory props between the individual and the concreteness of human intercourse creates, like Robert Frost's walls, divisions between human beings. "What man needs," according to Sartre, "is to find himself again and to understand that nothing can save himself, not even valid proof of the existence of God."[11] *Tiny Alice*, first staged during the Christmas season, is Albee's image of what Saul Bellow calls "the spiritual profile of the U.S.A."[12] The final irony in *Tiny Alice* concerns Julian's finding "himself again," but only within a universe whose mysteries define the inscrutability of God and the reality of death.

BETRAYALS

A Delicate Balance

A Delicate Balance is Albee's most blatant staging of the existentialist predicament. He does not chart cataclysmic changes; rather, he intimates the subtle shifts in human relationships, shifts from engagement to habit, from commitment to estrangement, from love to indifference. The play concerns the way in which "we submerge our truths and have our sunsets on untroubled waters,"[13] a pattern by now assuming a thematically preeminent position within Albee's aesthetic. The plot's lack of action perfectly captures the spiritual inertia that has gradually ossified this family. Consciousness comes too late, it seems, for by the play's closure Agnes and Tobias's awareness reveals a Nothingness, a void, nil. Agnes acknowledges this sense of wasted opportunity:

Everything becomes . . . too late, finally. You know it's going on . . . up on the hill; you can see the dust, and hear the cries, and the steel . . . but you wait; and time happens. When you *do* go, sword, shield . . . finally . . . there's nothing there . . . save rust; bones; and the wind (164).

Albee discussed the sense of wasted opportunities within *A Delicate Balance*:

Agnes says it in the third act of *A Delicate Balance* with

the metaphor of the battle going on up the hill; that you wait and when you do go it's all over. People find out about their lives, too. What could be worse than ending your life with regret about what you haven't done and end up your entire life realizing that you haven't participated? What could be worse?[14]

A Delicate Balance, first performed at the Martin Beck Theatre, New York City, 12 September 1966, signaled Albee's return to critical favor after his disastrous adaptation of James Purdy's *Malcolm* in January of 1966. *A Delicate Balance* went on to capture a Pulitzer Prize. The play concerns Agnes and Tobias, a couple nearing their sixties whose comfortable suburban life seems as well ordered as it is fulfilled. But Claire, Agnes's alcoholic sister who lives with the couple, Julia, their often-divorced daughter, and Harry and Edna, the family's best friends who move in because of their "terror," upset the complacent home. The unexpected and largely unwanted intrusions of these characters force Agnes and Tobias to reassess the nature of their love, their values, indeed their very existence. However, as the play closes, Albee ironically suggests that Agnes and Tobias willingly accept the failure of their own individual nerve; accept what essentially has developed into a death-in-life manner of living. Thus, *A Delicate Balance* presents a sense of aloneness in the midst of company, dread in the common, terror in the real. Moreover, the characters fail to salvage their lives in qualitative terms; at best Agnes and Tobias realize their condition too late. As Albee remarked, "But by the time Tobias is able to take a stand and make a choice and say 'yes, and come live with us,' the opportunity, the options have been removed from him. He can't do it . . . and so the terror in the play is about waste, yes, waste."[15] The play largely concerns forms of waste, then: wasted marriages, familial relations, whole existences.

Each character struggles with some form of terror, a sense of dread repressed until Harry and Edna upset the delicate balance by admitting their fear:

> *Harry* (*Looks at Edna*): I . . . I don't know quite what happened then; we . . . we were . . . it was all very quiet, and we were all alone . . . (*Edna begins to weep, quietly; Agnes notices, the others do not; Agnes does nothing*) . . . and then . . . nothing happened, but . . . (*Edna is crying more openly now*) . . . nothing at all happened, but . . .
> *Edna* (*Open weeping; loud*): WE GOT . . . FRIGHT-ENED. (*Open sobbing; no one moves*)
> *Harry* (*Quiet wonder, confusion*): We got scared.
> *Edna* (*Through her sobbing*): WE WERE . . . FRIGHT-ENED.
> *Harry*: There was nothing . . . but we were very

scared. (*Agnes comforts Edna, who is in free sobbing anguish. Claire lies slowly back on the floor*)
Edna: We . . . were . . . terrified.
Harry: We were scared. (*Silence; Agnes comforting Edna. Harry stock still. Quite innocent, almost childlike*)
It was like being lost: very young again, with the dark, and lost. There was no . . . thing . . . to be . . . frightened of, but . . .
Edna (*Tears; quiet hysteria*): WE WERE FRIGHTENED . . . AND THERE WAS NOTHING (45–47).

The existential authenticity of Harry and Edna's confession seems vague yet felt, vague because they cannot concretize their uneasiness, felt because they are frightened about their very being in the world. William Barrett, in *What Is Existentialism?*, discusses Martin Heidegger's *Angst*, which correlates precisely with Harry and Edna's condition as well as with Albee's overall thematic concerns in the play:

Anxiety (*Angst*) is the fundamental feeling precisely because it is directed toward the world more plainly than any other feeling. Anxiety is indefinite: it is not about this or that object, we are simply anxious and we do not know about what; and when it is over, we have to say that "it was about nothing." This is what the psychoanalysts call free-floating anxiety; anxiety without any discoverable object. . . . What we are anxious about in such states, Heidegger tells us, is our very Being-in-the-world as such. That is why anxiety

is more fundamental to human existence than fear.
Fear is always definite; about this or that object in the
world; but anxiety is directed toward our Being-in-the-
world itself, with which every definite object, or
thing, within the world is involved. Thus anxiety,
more than any other feeling, discovers to us the
world: i.e., brings us face to face with a world, to
which we now sense ourselves to be in precarious relation.[16]

Harry and Edna's uninvited anxiety disturbs the
characters' sense of well-being, forcing them to
sense the precariousness of their being in the
world. Harry and Edna's intrusion forces Tobias,
for one, to question his Daddy-like apathy. As
Barrett argues:

But in ordinary life we usually evade the condition:
we try to transform this indefinite anxiety into a definite fear or worry about this or that particular object.
Thus authentic anxiety disappears, in our banal existence . . . a state in which man perpetually busies himself with diversions and distractions from himself and
his own existence.[17]

Barrett describes the banality of those—as T. S.
Eliot writes in *Four Quartets*—"Distracted from distraction by distraction."[18] But Harry and Edna's
terror undermines the flaccidity of Agnes and
Tobias's family. "Anxiety," writes Barrett, "thus
gives us the first clue to an authentic existence

possible for the human person."[19] Their suprise invasion, like Elizabeth and Oscar's unexpected arrival in Sam and Jo's home in *The Lady from Dubuque*, triggers a consciousness that comes too late for Agnes and Tobias.

The anxiety and wasted potential embodied in *A Delicate Balance* surface through the self-government of the players. Claire seems the most honest, and perhaps the most perspicacious, character, despite her alcoholism. Her account of the horrors of her addiction, moreover, testifies to an honest awareness of her personal form of terror. Her vivid speech matches the intensity of Jerry's stories in *The Zoo Story*:

Pretend you're very sick, Tobias, like you were with the stomach business, but pretend you feel your insides are all green, and stink, and mixed up, and your eyes hurt and you're half deaf and your brain keeps turning off, and you've got peripheral neuritis and you can hardly walk and you hate. You hate with the same stinking sickness you feel your bowels have turned into . . . yourself, and *everybody*. Hate, and, oh, God!! you want love, l-o-v-e, so badly—comfort and snuggling is what you really mean, of course— but you hate, and you notice—with a sort of detachment that amuses you, you think—that you're more like an animal every day . . . you snarl, and *grab* for things, and hide things and forget where you hide them like not-very-bright dogs, and you wash less,

BETRAYALS

prefer to *be* washed, and once or twice you've actually soiled your bed and laid in it because you can't get up . . . pretend all that. No, you don't like that, Tobias? (23).

Although Claire is the "stereotypic wise drunk" moving "uncertainly through the play making wise cracks,"[20] her often-accurate appraisals provide a healthy contrast to Tobias's wafflings, Harry and Edna's vagueness, Julia's childishness, and Agnes's orderliness.

Claire is direct. She can identify the most conspicuous absence in the family—the lack of love. Eloquently blunt, she gains the audience's attention, and perhaps admiration, by slicing through the irritating rhetorical gallantries of Agnes and the banal cackle of Tobias. Despite her frivolity and humor—the swim suit story, her hamming with the accordion, the flippant one-liners—Claire seems disarmingly honest. Because "we live with our truths in the grassy bottom," Claire explains, "we better develop gills" (93). Her reference to gills suggests a way of adapting to and surviving a confusing reality. As Ronald Hayman points out, "Generally [Albee] uses Claire rather like a Shakespearean fool. She penetrates fearlessly, if drunkenly, to the central truths. . . . She can therefore afford to be honest about the facts of her own life and to probe rudely into facts of other people's."[21] Though she will never sustain a meaningful relationship, Claire values engagement. But her awareness finally merely accentuates her own sense of loss; she is intelligent enough to pinpoint personal anxieties but lacks the wherewithal to change.

Her lack, an inability to use adaptive "gills," so pervades her life that she emerges as impotent as Julia or Tobias. Drinking neutralizes her impulse to live. She may be the least susceptible to the Hemingway-like dread, but what she gains through her purported resilience seems lost through the half-life she lives: she is one of "the walking wounded" (152). Desiring love and companionship, she never enters into meaningful relationships, so, as Jerry from *The Zoo Story* laments, "What is gained is loss." Commitment to anything beyond a drink seems unmanageable. On one level her detachment from the others helps. "Sidelines! Good seats, right on the fifty-yard line, objective observer" (72). Her role as objective observer gives her sufficient emotional distance from familial tensions. Seen from a different angle, however, her role also functions as a social buffer neatly preventing involvement in vital familial relationships. Claire exhibits no genuine pledge of commitment, prompting Agnes's telling remark, "How simple it is from the sidelines" (88). Claire, who "has never missed a chance to participate in watching" (135), seldom benefits from her disinterested interest, thus failing in the pragmatics of human communication, her insightful comment one moment negated by her subterfuge or by her lack of resolve the next.

While Claire is the uninvolved adult, Julia remains the thirty-six-year-old confused child. She is old enough to have ventured in and out of three (and probably four) marriages, yet young enough to demand, or need, parental pampering. Like Martha in *Who's Afraid of Virginia Woolf?* Julia's troubled past emotionally cripples her present world. Seeking shelter in her childhood home, she returns to find that Harry and Edna have usurped her room, and their occupation is a mark of rejection to her. Throughout much of the play she appears in "controlled hysteria" (54). In *A Delicate Balance* a room of one's own will not soothe her psychic scars. Julia's old home, Anne Paolucci observes, becomes "a mirage, a long-lost dream, the dead past, and in choosing to return to it, Julia is merely aggravating her already serious emotional difficulties."[22] Her failed marriages only increase her emotional dependency on her parents. An inability to order her life forces the homecoming, an ill-fated effort to locate her identity.

Parental rejection exacerbates Julia's sense of

abandonment. In her youth she felt neglected after getting "over my two-year burn at suddenly having a brother" (63). Immediately following Teddy's death she sensed an opportunity to regain her parents' recognition: she would come home "all bloody" (102), her skinned knees a deliberate attempt to win back her parents' love. As a teenager, she continued the disturbing pattern. Exiled to boarding school, she skinned her knees in a different way, deliberately failing courses as a way to return to what she hoped would be a loving home. Now that she is an adult, the pattern remains. She dissolves her marriages, surely in part because of incompatibility, but also, perhaps, because she still yearns subconsciously for her parents' love.[23] While her tantrums are socially immature, her outbursts become more understandable once we realize their psychological underpinnings. She "strikes out at Tobias as the author of the soap opera her life has become," as M. Gilbert Porter writes,[24] because she has lost psychic balance through the years of feeling abandoned.

The familial tensions stretch Julia's already unstable condition to its limits. She endures Claire's snide remarks, stumbles at her parents' judgments, and breaks when Harry and Edna usurp her room:

BETRAYALS

Edna (Calm): You may lie down in *our* room, if you prefer.
Julia (A trapped woman, surrounded): *Your* room! (*To Agnes*): *Your* room? MINE!! (*Looks from one to another, sees only waiting faces*) MINE!! (99).

Julia's room stands as a last symbolic connection with some vestige of security. The strangers occupying the room overwhelm her; the tonal quality of her language—she begins talking as a child would, calling for "Daddy"—is indicative of her psychic vertigo, her collapse of nerve. Home for emotional succor and replenishment, she discovers only additional rejection. At one point she appears trapped in the throes of a nervous breakdown:

(*Julia appears in the archway, unseen by the others; her hair is wild, her face is tear-streaked; she carries Tobias' pistol, but not pointed; awkwardly and facing down*) *Julia (Solemnly and tearfully)*: Get them out of here, Daddy, getthemoutofheregetthemoutofheregetthem outofheregetthemoutofheregetthemoutofhere (113).

Her collapse only begets further wrath: Agnes wants her "horsewhipped" and exclaims, "How dare you embarrass me and your father! How dare you frighten Edna and Harry! How dare you come into this room like that!" (114). Godmother Edna supplies the *coup de grace* by slapping her. Reduced to a "confused child" (117), her terrifying fear of abandonment reconfirmed, Julia exits, shattered.

Agnes is the delicate balancer. She emerges as the one capable of pinpointing articulately the loss of will, the nonlove, and takes on the responsibility of imposing some coherence within her family. Her strength of being stems from her ability to deal with raising and counseling Julia; with rescuing Claire from binges; with the death of her second child; with Tobias's capitulation to a death-in-life existence. She concedes certain hubristic faults, although such flaws are products of leadership qualities:

If I am a stickler on points of manners, timing, tact— the graces, I almost blush to call them—it is simply that I am the one member of this . . . reasonably happy family blessed and burdened with the ability to view a situation objectively while I am in it.[. . .] There *is* balance to be maintained, after all, though the rest of you teeter, unconcerned, or uncaring, *assuming* you're on level ground . . . by divine right, I gather, though that is hardly so. And if I must be the fulcrum . . . (81–82).

She valiantly tries facing the facts of their all-too-human conditions. Rising above the indifference or perverse anger of her family, Agnes struggles to maintain the dynamics of her family. Her self-appointed generalship invites Laura Julier to observe, "Albee focuses more on her inner strength than on her power."[25]

However, Agnes's effort to "keep *it* from falling apart" (80) ironically promotes the family's spiritual inertia. Maintaining delicate balance within this play means sustaining an entropic present. Even the preciosity of her speech patterns—the highly mannered cadences—suggests not merely her method of preserving sanity by articulate sheer will but also her way of gaining the upper hand with others. Language, for Agnes, becomes a manipulative more than communicative vehicle. John J. von Szeliski believes Agnes's language "has been a handy substitute for an ability to love or to enforce a decision based on love—and it has also been a wonderful subconscious weapon for domination."[26] Virginia I. Perry points out that Agnes's language also correlates to the illusion of her well-being: "Verbal dexterity is Agnes' weapon against what she cannot understand, articulateness her mooring in the world."[27] Thus her social strategy evolves into a corrosive force as devastating as the withdrawals of Peter in *The Zoo Story* or Julian in *Tiny Alice* or the Son in *All Over.* Her maintenance generates stasis. Her attitudes and assumptions neatly preserve what Eliot in *Four Quartets* calls "the mental emptiness" paralyzing her family. Albee heightens the sense of waste in that Agnes seems intelligent enough to discern fundamental public issues and private tensions—

but does nothing about them. Rather, Albee implies, she sells out to a cushioned bourgeois existence: "There are no mountains in my life . . . nor chasms. It is a rolling, pleasant land . . . verdant, my darling, thank you" (9). She perceives terror, which ushers forth a moment of crux in her life, only to revert—through language—to the comfortable holding pattern characterizing her world. As Albee observes, "Anges and Tobias in *A Delicate Balance* realize they can't handle the precipice."[28] Hence, M. Patricia Fumerton correctly concludes, language "forms an impenetrable blockage, a thick layer of skin within which each individual may rest secure: isolated and lonely and—tragically—invulnerable."[29]

The exhilarating language of Albee's plays before *A Delicate Balance* often reflected a liberating force, a means by which the individual communicated meaning directly with another person. From *A Delicate Balance* onward, however, language tends to conceal rather than reveal, the splits between words, meanings, and deeds becoming noticeably larger. Thematically the language his characters invent not only defines but confines their very place within the world. Language entraps as much as it explains.

Albee demonstrates the extent to which language entraps through Tobias. Apparently

BETRAYALS

Tobias's material comforts blunt ambition, the luxury of servants and country clubs filling the vacant spaces created by his unwillingness to communicate with a sense of urgency or purpose. But he is not Albee's latest version of an emasculated Daddy figure, in part because the author develops his character more completely, but also because Tobias himself elects consciously to withdraw from the complex business of living. Like Charlie in *Seascape*, he is a victim of his self-imposed exile from commitment. Inertia, not strength of will, carries Tobias into his sixties. He wants his well-ordered world untroubled—"Just let it be" (60)—so he can nurture the calm civility of his home, the illusion of his love.

Two important events psychically jolted Tobias: the deaths of the cat and of Teddy, his son. In the story of the cat, Tobias recalls his intense relationship with the animal and her lack of love. Somewhat like the narrator in Poe's "The Black Cat," Tobias became "*fixed* on" the animal (35), thus sealing her doom: "I had her *killed!*" (36). And, like Poe's narrator, Tobias feels haunted by the cat's death. Symbolically the story of the cat correlates to the lack of love in Tobias's world, for just as the cat responded indifferently to him, so Tobias responded indifferently to Agnes and Julia. Just as Julia tried winning her father's affection, so Tobias tried earning his cat's attention, unsuccessfully. In brief, he felt *"betrayed"* (36) by the cat. The trauma of his relationship with the cat and her murder began his emotional withdrawal from human encounters.

If his marriage and prosperity helped Tobias's recovery, the death of Teddy soon after birth irrevocably plunged him into psychic imprisonment. His self-ordered celibacy for some thirty years signifies much more than sexual disinterest; it's the outward form of a complete internal retreat from any risk taking, from any kind of significant human engagement. An affair with Claire immediately following his son's death does not fill the void; Julia obviously cannot replace Teddy; even Agnes cannot restore his physical or spiritual vitality. Rather than risk another loss he becomes remote, detached, a man whose "mind is conscious of nothing," to borrow Eliot's phrase.[30] A generation later Agnes recalls his descent into indifference:

> I think it was a year, when you spilled yourself on my belly, sir? "Please? Please, Tobias?" No, you wouldn't even say it out: I don't want another child, another loss. "Please? Please, Tobias?" And guiding you, *trying* to hold you in?
> *Tobias (Tortured):* Oh, Agnes! Please!
> *Agnes:* "Don't leave me then, like that. Not again,

> Tobias. Please? *I* can take care of it: we *won't* have
> another child, but please don't . . . leave me like
> that." Such . . . silent . . . sad, disgusted . . . love
> (137–38).

Unable to face another possible loss, Tobias enam-
els his emotions. Over the years, in Porter's words,
"Tobias lets his inaction imply his working creed:
nothing ventured, nothing lost."[31] Tobias contributes to the family's illusion of equilibrium simply
by not being there; he fails in what Heidegger
meant by *Dasein*, or the state of being fully present
to one's place within the world. He is a total
"stranger" (123), even to his own wife.

Harry and Edna ignite his awakening. Unchar-
acteristically vocal, Tobias accepts the terror his
guests bring: "YOU BRING YOUR PLAGUE! YOU
STAY WITH US! I DON'T WANT YOU HERE! I
DON'T LOVE YOU! BUT BY GOD . . . YOU
STAY!! (162). Such an awakening, however, does
not lead to a definitive change. With Agnes, he
realizes their lives have been wasted, and his
climatic ravings near the play's end merely serve as
a painful reminder of the wasted opportunities, of
the emptiness of his life.

A positive reading of Agnes's closing speech
might suggest the possibility of regeneration.
Maybe Tobias and Agnes will, like George and
Martha before them, live more honestly "when

daylight comes again" (170). A bleaker reading of the end, however, seems more in accord with Albee's thematic concerns. Both Agnes and Tobias have the chance to confront the illusions governing their world, Tobias' epiphanic litany at the end signaling a qualitative shift from an anesthetized stance to a state of aliveness. But they consciously choose to maintain the delicate balance which tragically preserves their vital lies.

Notes

1. Edward Albee, author's note, *Tiny Alice* (New York: Atheneum, 1965). The page references within the text are to this edition.

2. Press conference transcript, Billy Rose Theatre, New York City, 22 March 1965. Quoted here from Richard E. Amacher, *Edward Albee*, rev. ed. (Boston: Twayne, 1982) 119–20.

3. William F. Lucey, "Albee's *Tiny Alice*: Truth and Appearance," *Renascence* 21 (1969): 79. See also Dennis Grunnes, "God and Albee: *Tiny Alice*," *Studies in American Drama, 1945–Present* 1 (1986): 61–71.

4. Mary E. Campbell, "The Tempters in Albee's *Tiny Alice*," *Modern Drama* 13 (1970): 25. See also Campbell's "The Statement of Edward Albee's *Tiny Alice*," *Papers on Language and Literature* 10 (1968): 85–100.

5. Edward Albee, *Counting the Ways and Listening* (New York: Atheneum, 1977) 110.

6. Anita Marie Stenz, *Edward Albee: The Poet of Loss* (The Hague: Mouton, 1978) 62.

7. Albert Camus, *The Myth of Sisyphus and Other Essays* (New York: Vintage, 1955) 10.

BETRAYALS

8. Mary Castiglie Anderson, "Staging the Unconscious: Edward Albee's *Tiny Alice*," *Renascence* 32 (1980): 189–90.

9. Thomas P. Adler, "Art or Craft: Language in the Plays of Albee's Second Decade," *Edward Albee: Planned Wilderness*, ed. Patricia De La Fuente, (Edinburg, TX: Pan American University Press, 1980) 55.

10. Press conference transcript, Amacher, 119.

11. Jean-Paul Sartre, from *Existentialism Is a Humanism*, *Existentialism*, ed. Robert C. Solomon (New York: Modern Library, 1974) 204–05.

12. Saul Bellow, *Him with His Foot in His Mouth and Other Stories* (New York: Harper, 1984) 36.

13. Edward Albee, *A Delicate Balance* (New York: Atheneum, 1966) 93. Page references within the text are to this edition.

14. Matthew C. Roudané, "Albee on Albee," *RE: Artes Liberales* 10 (1984): 4.

15. Personal interview with the author, 23 Sept. 1980, Berkeley, CA.

16. William Barrett, *What Is Existentialism?* (New York: Grove, 1964) 58–59.

17. Barrett 59.

18. T. S. Eliot, *The Complete Poems and Plays* (New York: Harcourt, Brace, 1971) 120.

19. Barrett 59.

20. C. W. E. Bigsby, *Albee* (Edinburgh: Oliver and Boyd, 1969) 107.

21. Ronald Hayman, *Edward Albee* (New York: Ungar, 1971) 102–03.

22. Anne Paolucci, *From Tension to Tonic: The Plays of Edward Albee* (Carbondale: Southern Illinois University Press, 1972) 110.

23. See Michael E. Rutenberg, *Edward Albee: Playwright in Protest* (New York: Avon, 1969) 136.

24. M. Gilbert Porter, "Toby's Last Stand: The Evanescence of Commitment in *A Delicate Balance*," *Educational Theatre Journal* 31 (1979): 403.

25. Laura Julier, "Faces to the Dawn: Female Characters in Albee's Plays," De La Fuente, 38.

26. John J. von Szeliski, "Albee: A Rare *Balance*," *Twentieth Centure Literature* 16 (1970): 126.

27. Virginia I. Perry, "Disturbing Our Sense of Well-Being: The 'Uninvited' in *A Delicate Balance*," *Edward Albee: An Interview and Essays* ed. Julian N. Wasserman, Lee Lecture Series, University of St. Thomas, Houston, TX (Syracuse: University of Syracuse Press, 1983) 59.

28. Roudané 4.

29. M. Patricia Fumerton, "Verbal Prisons: The Language of Albee's *A Delicate Balance*," *English Studies in Canada* 7 (1981): 210.

30. Eliot 126.

31. Porter 399.

CHAPTER FIVE

Death and Life:
All Over and *Seascape*

In his *Fools of Time: Studies in Shakespearean Tragedy*, Northrop Frye writes that death is "the essential event that gives shape and form to life. Death is what defines the individual, and marks him off from the continuity of life that flows indefinitely between the past and the future."[1] After *Breakfast at Tiffany's* (1966), a musical based on Truman Capote's book, *Everything in the Garden* (1968), an adaptation of Giles Cooper's play, and the inventive companion plays, *Box* and *Quotations from Chairman Mao Tse-Tsung* (1968), the next Albee work was *All Over*, a play whose subject matter revolves around death, the essential event. The reality of death forms the shaping principle of the drama, which was first staged at the Martin Beck Theatre, New York City, on 27 March 1971. Albee's working title for the play was simply *Death*.[2] His real concern is not death, however, but the kinds of existentialist pressures death exerts on those still living. Albee reconnoiters a psychic terrain, as tempered by the dying man, of those remaining. Thematically *All Over* extends the author's absorption with individual and social responses toward death and dying. As the Long-Winded Lady puts it in *Quotations from Chairman Mao Tse-Tung*, "Death is nothing; there . . . there *is* no death. There is only life and dying."[3]

In terms of story and plot, not much happens. All the characters congregate around a famous man who is dying, forming a socially awkward death watch. Social awkwardnesses stem from the various characters' psychohistories. Each character's past forms a subtle but important part of a larger whole; the play's real subject matter, it turns out, deals with the petty deceits and minor betrayals which, over the course of a lifetime, have grown into nothing less than a death-in-life pattern of existence. The play ends with the famous man's death, but Albee implies that it has been "all over" for the living characters for too long.

Elisabeth Kübler-Ross's theories influenced Albee while composing *All Over*. Her research on familial and cultural reactions to death, published two years before *All Over*, centers on the unique stresses both the living and the dying experience psychologically during the various stages of the dying process. Among her complex findings she voices a simple observation that could well serve,

DEATH AND LIFE

in dramatic terms, as Albee's point of departure: "The dying patient's problems come to an end, but the family's problems go on."[4] Albee's interest lies well beyond the dying man, for what strikes us most forcibly about the play is the other characters' problems and their responses, not so much toward the dying man, but toward themselves. Albee's concern, furthermore, is not with what happens, but why.

The "why" is revealed through the play's structure and set. The action occurs in the dying man's home, but Albee quickly calls into question the expected security and warmth of the home environment because "its cold spotlights and brilliant metallic furniture" convey "the atmosphere of a high black vault."[5] He further minimizes the humanness of the situation by describing the dying man as if he were an octopuslike machine: "the body of the beast, the tentacles, electrical controls, recorders, modulators, breath and heart and brain waves, and the tubes!, in either arm and in the nostrils."[6] Within this set Albee structures the dialogue so that each character's past history, always in relation to the dying man, is brought into relief, producing a composite image of mostly failed or frustrated relationships. This is a family united through the dying man, their gathering by necessity a civic as well as personal ritual of mourning and reminiscing, a cultural and private way to gain collective energy during the death vigil. But what emerges during the man's last two hours seems anything but unifying, for Albee presents familial schisms, disassociations, dissonances. Any mythic or regenerative powers implicit in such a family reunion become lost, the artificiality and tensions of the occasion rivaling the reality of death. Issues of adultery, rejections, withdrawals surface as the individual existences of the characters intersect. Despite the tremendous influence the dying man apparently exerted throughout his life on those within his orbit, each character ultimately seems unwilling or incapable of celebrating anything external to the self. Their selfishness overshadows the dying man's predicament. Throughout *All Over*, Albee presents the tension of the situation, the strained psychodynamics between the characters, and, perhaps most importantly, the way in which each individual interprets reality only as it applies to his or her own personal opportunities. "It is a play about the excluding self," C. W. E. Bigsby points out, "about that rigorous egotism which Albee sees as lying at the heart of human action."[7]

Within *All Over* the egocentric interests of the characters so infiltrate their motives and language that such human values as love and compassion

DEATH AND LIFE

fade, become distant social forces. A special kind of death replaces such humanistic values: not the physical disintegration of body but the metaphysical dissolution of the individual spirit. The death-in-life motif, so prevalent in the early plays, continues in *All Over* and the subsequent plays. As Robbie Odom Moses writes, "Death in this play encompasses those who have died, those who are dying, and those who *are* dead to life."[8] Albee accentuates the deadness of the characters by denying them names; their namelessness, juxtaposed with their formidable egos, contributes to the audience's perception that each family member is alienated from the others.

The Son and the Daughter embody all the wasted potential Albee seems fixed on dramatizing. The Son, a Tobias-like figure, views his job as a convenient distraction, although he admits his uselessness within the firm and merely goes through the motions as "a way of getting through from ten to six, and avoiding all I know I'd be doing if I didn't have it . . . (*Smiles a bit*) those demons of mine" (60). Perhaps his father's dying evokes genuine grieving or honest reflection, but the Son's awareness of loss, like Agnes's in *A Delicate Balance*, comes too late. A variation of the emasculated Daddy-figure, the Son willingly accepts his anesthetizing routines. The Daughter complements her brother, as she appears similarly entrapped in her version of a death-in-life world. She differs from her brother in her pent-up rage and is closer in temperament to Julia of *A Delicate Balance*. The Daughter is the rejected, confused child venting her personal setbacks by verbally attacking, by projecting her inner anxieties on her mother—"You make me as sick as I make you" (83)—and the Mistress. At the end of act 1, after the Wife and the Mistress join forces in their berating of the Daughter, she screams repeatedly, *"You fucking bitches!"* (48). This explains why one of her principal cares, as she admits to her brother, is how much "guilt I can produce in those that do the hurting" (62). Embodiments of inertia and anger, the Son and the Daughter, the inheritors of the famous man's legacy, are fitting symbols of the play's death motif.

The Nurse, the Doctor, and the Best Friend, despite their well-meaning intentions, cannot counterbalance the egotism pervading *All Over*. For example, the Best Friend appears as impotent as the Son and as ineffectual as the Daughter, especially in light of the lurid events of his past—the affair with the Wife, how he contributed to his own wife's insanity—events signaling the start of his own forty-year pattern of calculated indifference.

DEATH AND LIFE

Clearly, then, a central theme of *All Over* concerns various kinds of loss, particularly the loss of love. The Mistress, throughout the drama, defines the differing ways in which love loses its potency. On an obvious level she experienced physical losses of love: both her husbands died unexpectedly—"heart attack, and car" (69). The Mistress can also locate an equally devastating form of death, the symbolic passing away of love between two individuals, a betrayal prompting a willful enameling of the self from the other:

It's when it happens calmly and in full command: the tiniest betrayal—nothing so calamitous as a lie held on to in the face of fact, or so niggling as a fantasy during the act of love, but in between—and it can be anything, or nearly nothing, except that it moves you back into yourself a little, the knowledge that all your sharing has been . . . (16).

To the Daughter the Mistress is an opportunist, the conspiring temptress who has loved for greed and money. And surely Albee's naming her the Mistress conjures images of a sly seductress (at least when she was in her early thirties, the age she would have been when she first met her famous suitor). But her thirty-year liaison with the famous man is grounded on more than money or sexual fulfillment, as the Daughter and perhaps the Wife would have it. Rather, Albee presents the Mistress as a woman who, like the speaker in John Donne's "Break of Day," values honest commitment and genuine love—even at the risk of social awkwardness. A wealthy woman long before meeting the famous man, she enters into a relationship out of desire, not need. She provides a corrective to the Daughter's unfounded reasons for their lifelong affair:

And I told your father I wanted nothing beyond his company . . . *and* love. He agreed with me, you'll be distressed to know, said *you needed* it. So. I am not your platinum blonde with the chewing gum and the sequined dress (70).

After seventy-one years of living the Mistress has developed a maturity and sensibility that allows her to rise, with some grace, above the Daughter's derisive attacks. Despite her outward composure, however, the Mistress agonizes throughout the play, for the dying process of her life-mate, unlike the sudden deaths of her past husbands, forces her to confront and accept her greatest loss. She will carry on but fears her future will lack clarity; everything will be "out of focus" (101).

The Wife confirms the extent of loss permeating *All Over*. She, more than the others, experi-

DEATH AND LIFE

ences the lack of love. Reviewing her seven decades of living, she recalls the past when she and her husband connected "with talk and presence" (19). The deathwatch, of course, reminds her of isolation, aloneness, the products of what has been essentially her nonmarriage. Like Agnes in *A Delicate Balance* she maintains the status quo—at the cost of living itself: "I've settled in to a life which is comfortable, interesting, and useful, and I contemplate no change" (102). The spoils of practicing "widowhood" (101) render the Wife incapable of changing the dismal patterns of her solitary world.

At the close of *All Over* the Wife addresses both the incompleteness and complexity of her life and marriage. Moments before the famous man dies, the Mistress tries bolstering the Wife emotionally: "Shhhhhhhhh; be a rock" (106). Whatever positive, strength-giving associations her reference to the rock provides pale in the face of the overwhelming reality of death, the finality of which certifies the Wife's loss of love. "*You* be; *you* be the rock," she firmly replies to her rival. "I've *been* one, for all the years; steady. It's profitless!" (107). The image of the rock thus turns into a telling emblem for the negative epiphany the Wife experiences. The rock gives off merely the illusion of strength and rootedness; but, as the Wife now admits, the rock image refers to the rigidity and stasis of her existence. Realizing her whole life has been as static and deadened as a rock, she ends the play with an outpouring of years of frustration. With a felt sense of loss, she denies loving any of the others. Estranged from her husband for a generation, she confesses her care for the one on whom she has remained fixed: "I LOVE MY HUS-BAND!!" (108). Albee plainly dramatizes the intensity of her purging release of emotion and misery:

(*It explodes from her, finally, all that has been pent up for thirty years. It is loud, broken by sobs and gulps of air; it is self-pitying and self-loathing; pain, and relief*) Because . . . I'm . . . unhappy. (*Pause*) Because . . . I'm . . . un-happy. (*Pause*) BECAUSE . . . I'M . . . UNHAPPY! (*A silence, as she regains control. Then she says it once more, almost conversational, but empty, flat*) Because I'm un-happy (110).

Until this outburst the Wife seems curiously accepting of those around her, her composure and rapprochement with the Mistress masking her terror. Her confession shatters the forced, artificial coherence cementing her world. More than defining personal vacancies, the Wife highlights the degree to which the family has certified their own losses through their self-serving interests:

All we've done . . . is think about ourselves. (*Pause*)

DEATH AND LIFE

There's no help for the dying. I suppose. Oh my; the burden. (*Pause*) What will become of *me* . . . and *me* . . . and *me*. (*Pause*) Well, we're the ones have got to go on. (*Pause*) Selfless love? *I* don't think so; we love to *be* loved, and when it's taken away . . . then why *not* rage . . . or pule. (*Pause*) All we've *done* is think about ourselves. Ultimately (109–10).

Perhaps the Wife's account of her aunt best captures the source of such egocentrism. Her aunt lived until the age of sixty-two, but "died when she was twenty-six—died in the heart, that is, or whatever portion of brain controls the spirit" (51). This is the surrender of the will, the deadening capitulation of one's vitality, a kind of spiritual malaise afflicting each character, in some cases for decades, in *All Over*.

Like Bessie in *The Death of Bessie Smith*, who is never seen in the play, the dying man never appears on stage in *All Over*. Yet like Bessie Smith, he asserts his presence throughout the play. His dying, ironically enough, gives definition to the others' lack of aliveness. Albee deliberately hides the famous man behind a screen, the symbolic separator of the dying patient from the living family members. The screen represents, for Albee as for Kübler-Ross, a disturbing cultural distancing response, a way to deny an unpleasant reality. The screen also reinforces the separation of man and wife, parent and child. Not once, for instance, do the Best Friend, the Son, the Daughter, the Wife, or the Mistress actually visit the dying man. Clearly the deathwatch ritual in this play never embodies authentic meaning for the characters; none gains any communal or individual energy or soothing. Each character has withdrawn from graspable human relationships and entered a dream world.

Albee reinforces the inactive spirit of the characters by having them exist as if they were partially anesthetized, living in a dream world. In text as in performance they often converse "languorously" (3) in act 1; by act 2 they are "dozing," and "exhaustion has overwhelmed them; even awake they seem to be in a dream state. What one says is not picked up at once by another" (57). Albee refers, in symbolic and dramatic terms, to a kind of dream world, a form of moral sleep which so appalled Thoreau and, closer to our time, Camus and Bellow. Such a relinquishment of the spirit is, for Albee, unacceptable. The playwright will rethink some of the broader thematic issues raised in *All Over*—the interplay of death, dying, and the manner of living—in his next and decidedly more optimistic work, *Seascape*.

DEATH AND LIFE

Seascape

Albee's theater challenges those who, as the playwright has said, "turn off" to the complex business of living, who "don't stay fully awake" in relationships, who for various reasons choose not to immerse themselves in an "absolutely full, dangerous participation" in experience.[9] *Seascape* once again reflects those thematic concerns to which Albee continually gravitates. In *Seascape* he explores three interwoven forces: animal nature, as imaged by the sea lizards Sarah and Leslie; human nature, as reflected by Nancy and Charlie; and the kind of existentialist imperative forged by the curious intermixing of the animal world with the human world. The audience discovers Albee's response to the fact that so many people turn off. Originally titled *Life*, the play reconfirms Albee's ongoing battle to stage the various kinds of ethical problems with which his heroes struggle, whether they know it or not—or even care to know.[10]

The design of *Seascape* seems simple enough. Nancy and Charlie are vacationing at the beach, where they have finished a picnic. They are relaxing, reminiscing, figuring out what they will do with their lives now that their children are grown and their own years are numbered. They give voice to different selves and motivations, but during their encounter with the sea lizards their purposes ultimately unite, fixing on a shared consciousness concerning, to go back to Jerry's words in *The Zoo Story*, "the way people exist with animals, and the way animals exist with each other, and with people too."[11] Their new-tempered awareness, as seen throughout the Albee canon, objectifies Albee's central concern.

Charlie contends that they have "earned a little" rest from the hectic business of living.[12] Nancy, however, rejects this notion. In spite of their successful marriage Charlie and Nancy, currently on the threshold of beginning a new life—retirement—disagree on the way in which they will live out their remaining years. As in so many of his earlier plays Albee again joins opposites as a method of producing dramatic tension. Charlie is passive and inert, Nancy active and alive. Charlie elects withdrawal, while Nancy seeks engagement. He resists, she persists. She acts as a kind of benevolent instructor, he as the indifferent student. Charlie is tired of living, seems bereft of emotion, while Nancy is eager to investigate new terrain, willingly embracing change. Both clearly want to relax, but their interpretations of relaxation clash. Nancy craves to use their new free time by traveling along the world's shoreline as "seaside nomads" (5), exploring the wondrous sights of the

DEATH AND LIFE

earth. For Nancy life becomes meaningful when one *lives* it. She may have, in her older age, slight physical handicaps, but she does not suffer from the disabling psychological wounds that paralyze so many Albee protagonists. Albee shows her exuberance, enthusiasm, and spiritual vitality:

I love the water, and I love the air, and the sand and the dunes and the beach grass, and the sunshine on all of it and the white clouds way off, and the sunsets and the noise that shells make in the waves and, oh, I love every bit of it, Charlie (5).

The first act presents Nancy's optimistic stance toward living, as the tonal quality of her language suggests. Unlike the tonal quality of language in, say, *Counting the Ways* and *Listening*, which seems so tortured that the act of viewing or reading often becomes difficult, the language in *Seascape* emanates a lighthearted, humorous quality. Nancy voices this quality. For example, as her rapture with travel dreams continues, she exclaims to her lethargic husband, "My God, Charlie: See Everything Twice!" (10). Albee's thematic point centers on portraying a wife concerned with her husband, with loving attempts to revitalize his spirit.

Charlie resists. He has "to be pushed into everything" (7) because, as he informs Nancy, "I don't want to travel from beach to beach, cliff to sand dune, see the races, count the flies" (8). Retirement for Charlie means he can rest—and do nothing. He seems in many ways reminiscent of Peter in *The Zoo Story*, Daddy in *The American Dream*, Tobias in *A Delicate Balance*, and the Son in *All Over*, for Charlie also elects to withdraw from authentic engagement: "I'm happy . . . doing . . . nothing" (8). More than retiring from work, Albee suggests, Charlie is retiring from life itself, his spiritual laziness a willful surrendering of self-freedom.

Charlie defends his position. Claiming that Nancy's adventuresomeness would lead to "some . . . illusion" (38), he believes that "there's comfort in settling in" to doing nothing (39). After all, Charlie argues, "I *have* been a good husband to you" (31), and this is apparently true. He courted and loved Nancy, and fathered her children—just as she desired. By all accounts he has been faithful and forthright, the dependable provider and parent. From his point of view, Charlie has earned the right to do nothing. For him the choice to withdraw suggests that the whole affair of traveling, of being alive like Nancy, is too bothersome. If in functioning in a middle-class society, if in his efforts to uphold appearances, Charlie's vitality has diminished, it has clearly been his own conscious choice.

DEATH AND LIFE

His attitude disturbs Nancy. They have not earned a little rest but, counters Nancy, "We've earned a little *life*, if you ask *me*" (37). She appears determined to begin anew, in qualitative terms, their life together. Nancy advocates what for the author is an important existentialist tenet when voicing her desire to experience life as fully as possible. Specifically she is aware of the finiteness of their existences: "We are *not* going to be around forever, Charlie, and you may *not* do nothing" (9). Nancy's zest for living, her impulse to respond, may remind the audience of Henry James's Lambert Strether, who, in *The Ambassadors*, confides to Bilham: "Live all you can; it's a mistake not to. It doesn't so much matter what you do in particular, so long as you have your life. If you haven't had that what *have* you had?"[13] Like Strether, Nancy feels her old age on a physical level but refuses to capitulate on a spiritual level; she too wishes to "live all you can." Because of her insight Nancy appears objectively open toward experience, and will try anything, as long as they "do *something*" (9). Her zest for living takes on a larger, more compelling dimension because her stance is not a product of philosophic intellection but emerges from the concreteness of her conviction to experience fully her surrounding. Even years ago when, just married, Charlie slipped into a period of psychological withdrawal from both Nancy and life itself (his "seven-month decline"), Nancy felt a driving impulse to live. As she said, "The deeper your inertia went, the more *I* felt alive" (21).

Albee dramatizes Nancy's passion for life throughout the play. This is comically as well as seriously presented when Nancy catches Charlie speaking of their relationship in the past tense. Nancy ardently believes that they are having "a good life," not that, as Charlie sometimes states, they have "had a good life" (34). For Nancy and Albee alike, it is more than semantic nitpicking. Rather, it points to a whole way of being. Charlie rationalizes, perhaps convincingly, that "it's a way of speaking!" but Nancy objects: "No! It's a way of thinking!" (35). Nancy exclaims that they now have "two things!" (36) left, namely, "ourselves and some time" (37). Aware of the significance and precariousness of these two precious elements— the self and time—Nancy squares her hopes on experiencing qualitatively the world external to her self. She appears innately opposed to the Tobias-like acquiescence that can neutralize the individual's impulse to live.

In the midst of their conversation during the waning moments of act 1 Nancy and Charlie encounter the two anthropomorphic, green-scaled

DEATH AND LIFE

sea lizards, Sarah and Leslie. At this point Albee begins accentuating Nancy's and Charlie's differing attitudes toward experience. He objectifies this difference by the couple's initial reaction to the sea lizards: Charlie panics, Nancy beckons. While he issues a call to arms—and brandishes a feeble stick—she gazes at the two creatures in awe, saying "They're magnificent!" (44). As the two imposing, curious sea lizards approach, Nancy takes peaceful command, assuming a submissive pose. Finally Charlie takes heed, holding his fright in check.

What follows, as in so many Albee plays, is the interacting of two distinct yet clearly related worlds—here represented by the human world and the animal world. The reader or viewer has witnessed this technique of joining two contrasting worlds before in the encounter of Peter and Jerry in *The Zoo Story*; in the contrast of Grandma's earlier values versus the newer values of Mommy and Daddy in *The Sandbox* and *The American Dream*; and in the meeting of the secular and the religious in *Tiny Alice*. In *Seascape* the yoking together of the human world and the sea lizard world provides a clear definition of Albee's thematic interest: that love and sharing and awareness are all necessary forces, forces to be integrated into one's inner reality if one is to live life honestly. But unlike some of Albee's earlier works, especially *All Over*, *Seascape* emphasizes the presence of love and sharing and awareness. In *Seascape* the bringing together of opposites—humans and sea lizards—does not produce illusions, deceit, or hatred. And it does not produce a Pyrrhic victory in which consciousness is gained, but with such terrible losses—alienation, suicide, murder, death—that the value seems dubious. Rather, the joining of Nancy and Charlie's world with that of Sarah and Leslie generates understanding, education, sharing, and love, perhaps at the cost of merely two bruised male egos.

Act 2 embodies the education of the characters. It starts simply enough, with Leslie and Sarah asking a barrage of questions ranging from the banal to the profound. As Charlie's fear and Nancy's confusion wear away, as Leslie's skepticism and Sarah's apprehension subside, the characters establish communication. As the difficulty of the questions increases, Nancy and Charlie fumble with imprecise explanations regarding birth and children—as when Nancy notes that humans keep their offspring for eighteen or twenty years because, she tells the uncomprehending sea lizards, "we *love* them" (86). Pressed to explain what love signifies, Nancy replies, "Love is one of the emotions" (87), to which an impatient Leslie retorts,

DEATH AND LIFE

"Define your terms. Honestly, the imprecision! You're so thoughtless!" (87). The two humans struggle to elaborate and to educate their companions about human life, as their reliance on abstract concepts suggests. But abstractions do not adequately account for the richness and complexity of actual experience. A frustrated Charlie turns the tables on the sea lizards by asking them about their past. What follows ostensibly concerns the sea lizards' account of their courtship. Through their honest and humorous tale of courtship, however, Sarah and Leslie reveal very humanlike emotions: love, hate, anger, hurt, jealousy. Leslie fought to win Sarah's affection; and this show of commitment forever united them, as Sarah remembers: "And there he *was* . . . and there *I* was . . . and here we *are*" (90). The exchange emerges as a point of illumination. For now Charlie provides a graspable illustration of the emotions and the way in which they function. He succeeds in making the abstract concrete.

Of all their discussions, from prejudice and bigotry to aerodynamics and photography, one topic appears crucial to the play. Nancy and Charlie have been discussing tools, art, mortality, those qualities and things which separate man "from the brute beast" (126), and again the concept of emotions, particularly love, surfaces. Charlie, miffed at Leslie's presence but wanting to show him the concrete reality of love, turns to Sarah. He pointedly asks what she would do if she lost Leslie. Her response:

> I'd . . . cry; I'd . . . I'd cry! I'd . . . I'd cry my eyes out! Oh . . . Leslie!
> *Leslie* (*Trying to comfort Sarah*): It's all right, Sarah!
> *Sarah*: I want to go back; I don't want to stay here any more. (*Wailing*) I want to go *back*! (*Trying to break away*) I want to go *back*! (129).

Here is Sarah's sudden experience of terror, her sense of aloneness, her understanding of the possibility of profound loss. The precariousness of her life with Leslie suddenly made real, Sarah is, for the first time, experiencing an awakening. Sarah's dread brings forth Leslie's emotions, and in the only violent scene in the play he attacks Charlie, the instinctive response to terror:

> *Leslie*: You made her cry! (*Hit*)
> *Charlie*: STOP IT!
> *Leslie*: I ought to tear you apart!
> *Charlie*: Oh my God! (*Leslie begins to choke Charlie, standing behind Charlie, his arms around Charlie's throat. It has a look of slow, massive inevitability, not fight and panic*) (131).

While communicating (and fighting), the characters reveal one of Albee's basic concerns in

DEATH AND LIFE

Seascape, namely, the importance and process of evolution. For the playwright is clearly rendering what occurs, in part at least, when the species evolves into a higher form of life. "Like Arthur Miller's somewhat similar allegory, *The Creation of the World and Other Business*," observes C. W. E. Bigsby, "*Seascape* is best regarded as a consciously naïve attempt to trace human imperfection to its source by unwinding the process of history and myth."[14] Sarah explains that their evolutionary process was caused by a sense of alienation: "We had a sense of not belonging any more " (116). As with most complex growth patterns, Albee suggests, their evolution did not occur in an epiphanic moment but developed over a longer period of time, reflecting a gradual coming to consciousness. In Sarah's words, "It was a growing thing, nothing abrupt" (116). This is not to suggest, however, that *Seascape* celebrates a naturalistic evolution, that it is simply a Darwinian pierce dramatizing the advancement of the saurians. Rather, the impact of Sarah and Leslie's realization of their estrangement from their familiar environment radically altered their perceptions not only of place, but of themselves within their natural place. Although she finds it difficult to articulate, Sarah still persists in her efforts to define their "sense of not belonging," even over Leslie's objections:

> . . . all of a sudden, everything . . . down there . . . was terribly . . . interesting, I suppose; but what did it have to do with *us* any more?
> *Leslie*: Don't Sarah.
> *Sarah*: And it wasn't . . . comfortable any more. I mean, after all, you make your nest, and accept a whole . .. array . . . of things . . . and . . . we didn't feel we *belonged* there any more. And . . . what were we going to do?! (116)

Leslie and Sarah have experienced the divorce between man and his environment that Albert Camus described as the "feeling of absurdity."[15] They have been experientially forced to question the whole of their existence. Further, the passage illustrates Albee's deft interweaving of a serious subject within a lighthearted context. In spite of the humor permeating much of the play, the scene presents the characters as quite earnest because Albee stages the effects of alienation. But whereas in the earlier plays alienation typically begot more estrangement, even death, here it gives way to a sense of belonging, a sense of community. Even a stubborn Charlie begins lowering his defenses, becoming shy one moment, enthusiastic the next, all in an effort to understand the sea lizards' process of evolution.

The theme of evolution continues with Nancy and Charlie's explanations. Charlie, for example,

DEATH AND LIFE

reflects on the origins of humankind, linking the sea lizards' home with his own environment:

> What do they call it . . . the primordial soup? the glop? That heartbreaking second when it all got together, the sugars and the acids and the ultraviolets, and the next thing you knew there were tangerines and string quartets. (118).

Besides suggesting a mere biological interpretation of humankind's development, Charlie and Nancy also connect human evolution with the sea lizard's animal evolution:

> Listen to this—there was a time when we *all* were down there, crawling around, and swimming and carrying on—remember how we read about it, Nancy? (118).

The comments transcend a report of biological history, for they also operate on an archetypal level, unifying the animal world with the human world. As Charlie figuratively sums up to a skeptical Leslie and a fascinated Sarah, "It means that once upon a time you and I lived down there" (119). Nancy carries on the discussion, saying that the primitive creatures of long ago necessarily evolved to a higher plane of existence because "they were dissatisfied" (121) with their lives, just as Sarah and Leslie were not "comfortable" any more with theirs.

The reader, of course, sees the parallels between the worlds of the two couples. As Sarah voices her displeasure with their lizard life "down there" (117), so Nancy voices her dissatisfaction with their human life on land. As the women are open and enthusiastic, the men are closed, skeptical. Both couples throughout the drama are upset by the loud jets that fly over the dunes. The two couples come to recognize and appreciate the similarities between their worlds, and through their questioning and answering they learn about much more than the biological origins and evolution of the species. In Albee's presentation they also learn about the evolution of the spirit.

The evolution of the spirit draws the two couples intimately together. Nancy and Charlie, and Sarah and Leslie not only play counterpoint to each other but also mirror each other. Sarah's confession that they "considered the pros and the cons. Making do down there or trying something else" (117) directly mirrors Nancy's admission that her life with Charlie needs reevaluation too. If Leslie exemplifies brute bestiality, Charlie's actions at times reflect precisely such animalistic behavior. Like their sea lizard counterparts the humans must try "something else" if their lives are to avoid the

DEATH AND LIFE

potential stagnation inherent in "resting" too much. What this means, Albee implies, is that they should immerse themselves in the shape and energy of experience itself.

In *A Delicate Balance*, Claire mentions the value of developing gills as a way of adapting to and surviving life. But for Claire and most others in *A Delicate Balance* such evolutionary capability functions as a means of coping with a confusing, puckish reality. The subterfuges in *A Delicate Balance* are not present in *Seascape*. Here humankind's ability to evolve, to use "gills" when needed, becomes necessary if the individual is to grow. Charlie argues this very point when discussing the value of one's capacity to evolve:

Mutate or perish. Let your tail drop off, change your spots, or maybe just your point of view. The dinosaurs knew a thing or two, but that was about it . . . great, enormous creatures, big as a diesel engine—(*To Leslie*) whatever that may be—leviathans! . . . with a brain the size of a lichee nut; couldn't cope, couldn't figure it all out; went down (123).

Albee further develops the connectedness of the humans and sea lizards when Charlie describes his boyhood immersions in the sea. Nancy even asks if he developed a fishlike form: "Gills, too?" (13). In one passage in the play Charlie lapses into a pleasurable recollection:

And I would go into the water, take two stones, as
large as I could manage, swim out a bit, tread, look
up one final time at the sky . . . relax . . . begin to go
down. Oh, twenty feet, fifteen, soft landing without a
sound, the white sand clouding up where your feet
touch, and all around you ferns . . . and lichen. You
can stay down there so long! You can build it up, and
last . . . so long, enough for the sand to settle and the
fish come back. And they do—come back—all sizes,
some slowly, eyeing past; some streak, and you think
for a moment they're larger than they are, sharks
maybe, but they never are, and one stops being an
intruder, finally—just one more object come to the
bottom, or living thing, part of the undulation and the
silence. It was very good (16–17).

As Sarah and Leslie explore the solid earth, so
Charlie, years ago, explored the sea. In both contexts sea creatures and humans are "eyeing past"
each other. Thematically, Charlie's recollection of
his submersion into the water directly correlates to
the obvious archetypal patterns embodied in *Seascape*.[16]

Returning to the sea, archetypalists tell us, is
one way for man to reestablish a rapport with the
natural cycle. It also symbolizes man's attempt to
reestablish contact with his own psyche. Carl Jung
wrote: "Water is no figure of speech, but a living
symbol of the dark psyche."[17] Although as a boy
Charlie could not intellectualize about his water

DEATH AND LIFE

experience, his account suggests that the immersion concretely placed him within his own dark psyche. In Charlie's account living on the surface was equated with "breakers" and "a storm, or a high wind"—chaotic forces which affected his external world. But "to go way down" to the cove's bottom, living underneath the surface, was equated with solitude and calming silence. Seeking adventure and a comforting refuge, Charlie established an intuitive, sympathetic correspondence with his self and the underworld. Jung discusses the influence of this kind of immersion:

The unconscious is the psyche that reaches down from the daylight of mentality and morally lucid consciousness into the nervous system that for ages has been known as the "sympathetic." This . . . maintains the balance of life and, through the mysterious pathways of sympathetic excitation, not only gives us knowledge of the innermost life of other beings but also has an inner effect upon them.[18]

In his underwater experience Charlie was privy to just this form of unique "knowledge of the innermost life." Thus, on an archetypal level Charlie's submersion allowed him to be present to his inner self, his hidden self, as well as to the world external to himself—the ocean world. Charlie's archetypal water experience serves as a rite of passage, a form of initiation into a primordial setting that precedes any capacity to evolve. In Jung's words, "The descent into the depths always seems to precede the ascent."[19]

But where is Charlie's "ascent"? Apparently his psychic ascent came long after his physical surfacing. As a teen-ager he came in touch with his inner psyche (16), but integrating the meaning of this experience is only achieved a lifetime later. In his unique encounter on the dunes Charlie rekindles contact with the natural cycle and with his self. Leslie and Sarah, of course, represent that vital contact. They represent what Charlie and Nancy were "eons" ago (117). As Lucina P. Gabbard points out, Leslie and Sarah "concretize the evolution of mankind from water animals, the emergence of the individual embryo from its watery womb, and the return to consciousness of the repressed self."[20] Thus, the random encounter of the two couples on the dunes symbolically reveals the connectedness of animal nature and human nature, the biological as well as spiritual kinship which exists, at least in this play, between beast and human.

The intermingling of the animal and human world in *Seascape*, finally, precipitates an existentialist imperative which has become a familiar

DEATH AND LIFE

trademark of any Albee play: the need to communicate authentically with the other. Through mutual communication the characters of *Seascape* evolve into what Jung calls a "higher consciousness."[21] In a state of higher consciousness Nancy voices one of Albee's central concerns in the play, saying, "And I'm aware of my own mortality" (125). Passing middle age, Nancy feels the nearness of death. For Charlie the nearness of death remains, like his childhood experience, distant. Only when Leslie nearly strangles him do Nancy's attitudes become tangible to Charlie. Through their collective experience the characters begin to understand and live with, in Albee's words, "the cleansing consciousness of death."[22] That is, the characters gain an acute awareness of the proximity of extinction, of the finiteness of their existence, which in turn creates the possibility for living life fully, as Nancy advocates throughout.

In spite of the evolving spirits of the characters, the mythical uniting of brute beast with civilized person, Albee does not formulate a purely fairy-tale ending: there is no guarantee that their lives will be substantially changed. Sarah, for example, shyly voices her concern surrounding evolution: "Is it . . . is it for the better?" and Charlie can only reply honestly: "I don't *know*" (124). The tentativeness evident in Charlie's response, like

George's "maybe" to Martha's questions at the close of *Who's Afraid of Virginia Woolf?* captures something of the precariousness of their newfound knowledge. But they discover that, with each other's compassion, they can help each other. As Leslie says in his play-closing line, "All right. Begin" (135).

If the couples learn anything during the play, Albee suggests that it involves the recognition of and the need for involvement, engagement, and love at a consciously aware level. Through their explanations of their respective roles on earth the couples come to view themselves in a larger context. If the sea lizards have much to learn about life "up here" (132), so, too, with the humans. Their struggle only highlights the archetypal circularity fusing the animal and human worlds. Nancy and Charlie realize that they are not "better" but are, perhaps, "more interesting" than animals (125); that they are but a more-developed link on the physical and spiritual evolutionary chain. Albee implies that through the sweep and play of evolutionary patterns humankind has transcended noble savagery and the instinctive response to nature, to become beings whose mentor increasingly is reason. Surely the power of reason, Albee would say, is useful, necessary; still, in *Seascape* the dominance of rational faculties poses a threat. The

DEATH AND LIFE

danger is that, with rationality triumphing over the instinctive, the primordial life-giving passions will dissipate, and, for Charlie at least, there will be no other source of vitality to replace them. Unless reason and the emotions exist in counterpoise, more will be lost in the wonders of evolution than gained. Albee implies that evolved humanity will cease to feel deeply, or, continuing to feel at all, the individual may care only for the wrong things. Perhaps this is why Albee has called *Seascape* "triste."[23]

Seascape, which opened on 26 January 1975 at the Sam S. Shubert Theatre, New York City, and which won Albee his second Pulitzer Prize, represents Albee's persistent concern with dramatizing what may occur if the human spirit withers. Here Albee is not writing merely about the naturalistic evolution of the human species, but about growth patterns of humankind, about combining the visceral and the intellectual into a new whole which is the consciously aware person.

Notes

1. Northrop Frye, *Fools of Time: Studies in Shakespearean Tragedy* (Toronto: University of Toronto Press, 1967) 3.

2. C. W. E. Bigsby, *A Critical Introduction to Twentieth-Century American Drama* (New York: Cambridge University Press, 1984) 2:318.

3. Edward Albee, *Box and Quotations from Chairman Mao Tse-Tung* (New York: Atheneum, 1969) 47–48.

4. Elisabeth Kübler-Ross, *On Death and Dying* (New York: Macmillan, 1970) 160.

5. Nelvin Vos, "The Process of Dying in the Plays of Edward Albee." *Educational Theatre Journal* 25 (1973): 80.

6. Edward Albee, *All Over* (New York: Atheneum, 1971) 9. Page references within the text are to this edition.

7. Bigsby 314.

8. Robbie Odom Moses, "Death as Mirror of Life: Edward Albee's *All Over*," *Modern Drama* 19 (1976): 74.

9. Matthew C. Roudané, "An Interview with Edward Albee," *Southern Humanities Review* 16 (1982): 41.

10. Bigsby, 318.

11. Edward Albee, *The Zoo Story* and *The American Dream* (New York: Signet, 1960) 39–40.

12. Edward Albee, *Seascape* (New York: Atheneum, 1975) 10. Page references within the text are to this edition.

13. Henry James, *The Ambassadors* (New York: Norton, 1964) 132.

14. Bigsby 318.

15. Albert Camus, *The Myth of Sisyphus and Other Essays* (New York: Vintage, 1955) 5.

16. For elaboration of the archetypal patterns in *Seascape*, see Thomas P. Adler, "Albee's *Seascape*: Humanity at the Second Threshold, "*Renascence* 31 (1979): 107–14; Lucina P. Gabbard, "Albee's *Seascape*: An Adult Fairy Tale," *Modern Drama* 21 (1978): 307–17; and Kitty Harris Smither, "A Dream of Dragons: Albee as Star Thrower in *Seascape*," *Edward Albee: Planned Wilderness*, ed. Patricia De La Fuente, (Edinburg, TX: Pan American University Press, 1980) 99–110.

17. Carl G. Jung, "Archetypes of the Collective Unconscious," *Twentieth Century Criticism*, ed. William J. Handy and Max R. Westbrook (New York: Free Press, 1974) 215.

18. Jung 217.

19. Jung 216.

20. Gabbard 308.

21. Jung 230. For further discussion of the role of consciousness

DEATH AND LIFE

in the play see Liam O. Purdon, "The Limits of Reason: *Seascape* as Psychic Metaphor," *Edward Albee: An Interview and Essays*, ed. Julian N. Wasserman, Lee Lecture Series, University of St. Thomas, Houston, TX (Syracuse: Syracuse University Press, 1983) 141–53.

22. Edward Albee, *The Plays* (New York: Coward, McCann, and Geoghegan, 1981) 1:10.

23. Matthew C. Roudané, "Albee on Albee," *RE: Artes Liberales* 10 (1984): 4.

CHAPTER SIX

Public Issues, Private Tensions: *The Lady from Dubuque* and *The Man Who Had Three Arms*

After *Seascape* Albee presented two relatively minor plays: *Listening*, which was first commissioned as a radio play for B.B.C. Radio Three and heard on 28 March 1976, and *Counting the Ways*, which had its American premiere (after its first performance at the National Theatre in London on 6 December 1976) at the Hartford Stage Company, Hartford, Connecticut, on 28 January 1977. His next Broadway drama was *The Lady from Dubuque*, a play which received what by this point in the playwright's career had become a familiar critical response: a great deal of scathing, scornful hostility and somewhat lesser amounts of praise.

The Lady from Dubuque, first performed in New York City at the Morosco Theater on 31 January 1980, focuses on vintage (indeed, some would say outworn) Albee themes—death, dying, and failed communication among the living. What makes the play engaging is its examination of how the central couple, Jo and Sam, ultimately respond to the complex process of living and dying. Through Sam and the other characters who are brought into the orbit of Jo's experience of dying, Albee suggests that, although Jo's life is physically about to cease, she radiates more life than do the physically healthy characters. Jo, in brief, is not the only character who is dying. Her companions, long before this play begins, have succumbed to a debilitating disease which now paralyzes them. Indeed, the spiritual malaise from which they suffer pervades *The Lady from Dubuque*, for throughout one finds an array of wasted relationships, wasted love, and even wasted lives.

Albee chronicles such waste through the two-act structure of the play. The first act serves chiefly to introduce and define the principal characters, whose painful vacuity and self-centeredness far overshadow any claim to individuality that each might make. Because each character becomes merely a hollow variation of a wasted life, the first act also serves to weld these types into a collective, a society of beings brought together through waste and mutual weakness. Having firmly established the normative values of this insular gathering, the playwright begins the second act by challenging those values through the introduction of two "alien" characters who are not of the world of the

first act. Within *The Lady from Dubuque* these outsiders, by providing Jo with the warmth and compassion that are absent in the first act, present a
threat which is ironically more strongly felt than
Jo's disease or the sense of mortality it may introduce into the various characters' lives.

Within the play's first act, what becomes most
apparent is not only the extreme lack of action but
also the lack of interaction. Each of the characters
speaks for himself but not to the others, so that the
game played in the first act appears as a type of
play within a play where the players adopt suitably
Pirandellian roles of self-conscious characters who
explain themselves directly to their supposed audience.

Fred surfaces as the clearest emblem of a
wasted life. His conduct and prejudice reveal a
dulled, coarsened sensibility. Foolish enough to be
duped by a practical joke in which Carol staves off
Sam's feigned entreaties, Fred responds in the only
fashion he knows: by physically asserting his presence. When threatened, Fred, according to stage
directions, characteristically readies himself "for
battle," resorting to verbal aggression and vulgar-
ity.[1] A few other telling scenes highlight Albee's
portrait. Near the end of the play a bound and
exasperated Sam screams, prompting Fred to arms

so that he punches his friend "hard in the stomach" (146), doubling Sam over in pain. Moments later Carol decides to have coffee, and Fred, threatened by her show of independence and reluctance to leave with him, "sweeps" the entire coffee service to the floor, shattering saucers, cups, and any claim to civility that he might have had (147).

Fred's propensity to assert himself physically suggests that for him reality is defined solely in terms of his own self-interest and by his severely limited, bigoted perceptions. He is more pathetic than, say, Eugene O'Neill's Yank, that image of raw, visceral man in *The Hairy Ape*, for the audience could at least empathize with Yank's struggle to "belong."[2] In contrast, the audience of *The Lady from Dubuque* can only recoil from Fred and his animality. This reaction occurs not because he is, in Jo's words, "just plain dirt common" (23), but because he treats those around him as objects rather than as human beings. Fred may be perceptive enough to ask, with respect to Sam and Jo's home, "Where else can you come in this cold world, week after week, as regular as patchwork, and be guaranteed ridicule and contempt?" (30), but he fails to see that he is the one creating dissonance. If his treatment of Carol is any indication, it is hardly surprising that he has been divorced three times. As Carol testifies, despite whatever sexual fulfillment she finds in Fred, he clearly provides little emotional or spiritual support. From the racial slurs with which he accosts Oscar (106) to the physical attack on his host (146), Fred consistently affirms his self-centeredness.

Carol emerges as a practical-minded woman. Described as young and "ripe," Carol considers marrying Fred, though she admits her uncertainty about Fred and matrimony. Because she remains confused about marriage, she quells her fear with simplistic reasoning: "I don't know, I don't know, I don't know! I know it's late and I got the itch, but beyond that I'm not sure" (38). Lacking in social refinement, Carol seems well matched with Fred. A woman who dyes her naturally blond hair brunette—"cause I look cheap as a blonde" (131)—Carol remains a comic figure, breaking certain tense scenes with her matter-of-fact and sometimes humorous lines.

As a newcomer to the group Carol enjoys a freedom from the long-established, deadening patterns of the others. Her role as an "outsider" (124) allows her to comment more honestly about their and her own responses. In certain respects she seems akin to Claire in *A Delicate Balance*: both appear outspoken, humorous, and capable of observing the others from a somewhat neutral vantage point, from the "fifty-yard line," as Claire says.[3] Like Claire, Carol also succumbs to her own emotional condition and seems unable ultimately to better herself.

If Carol is "not your dumb brunette" (131), it is because of her genuine, if limited, ability to be aware of the world around her. Unlike the others, her ego does not prevent her from experiencing the world apart from her self. Her judgment of character is surely flawed, for a relationship with Fred seems earmarked for failure. Still, Carol radiates an openness that distinguishes her from the others and gains for her the audience's sympathy. For example, Carol's only game of the night—the practical joke carried out with Sam—is truly engaging. It stands in marked contrast to the others' identity-guessing game of Twenty Questions, in which Carol chooses not to act out a part. Albee confirms Carol's openness in act 2 when she alone comes to Sam's defense. While the others question Sam's credibility, the newcomer, Carol, counters: "Why doesn't anybody believe *Sam*?" (125); "*Sam* has rights, you know" (134). Appropriately enough, she unties Sam near the close of the play.

For Carol, however, waste looms because she reduces her needs to relatively simple and confining terms. She neither requests nor receives much. If she is open, sharing, and honest, she also fails to improve her predicament, succumbing as she does to Fred's demands. Her obedience to Fred's callous requests foreshadows her final acquiescence to a wasted life, a surrender confirmed when she confides to Elizabeth her reasons for marrying Fred:

He's on his way downhill; he's a barrel of laughs; he's a lush; he's a great fuck; I'm not doing anything else this week; I'm not twenty-two anymore, and I'm scared? Take your choice; they're all true (151).

For Lucinda and Edgar the events of the evening represent part of a larger, repetitive routine. As usual, they visit Jo and Sam more out of habit than authentic concern. A former collegemate of Jo, Lucinda has settled into being Edgar's housewife. Polite and quick to observe propriety, she attends to social appearances, interjecting the banal or predictable remark when appropriate. Though Edgar confesses that they have "as much ridicule and contempt as the next house" (31), Lucinda objects, not because they do not battle as George and Martha did in *Who's Afraid of Virginia Woolf?* but simply because they do not communicate "with talk and presence," as the Wife in *All Over* recalls about her early life with her husband.[4] Lucinda's life, in accordance with her values, has been an untroubled one. Consequently when Jo berates her, she is hardly equipped to defend her values and convictions. After being ignored and then dismissed by Jo as essentially a bore—"You're lucky you've got anybody living in the same *house* with you, much less *talking* to you" (41)—Lucinda loses all emotional control. Edgar reports that "Lucinda's down there on the lawn, and she's pulling up tufts of grass and throwing 'em around, and she's got dirt all over her, and I don't think it's any crap" (52). In her opportunity to cut through the cackle and communicate honestly with her dying friend, Lucinda fails, choosing instead to exit and pout. It is her way of asserting that she, not Jo, suffers. And like Fred she never really attends to Jo. She knows that Jo's derisive behavior stems from a debilitating illness and yet bases her forgiveness of Jo, not on genuine care or love, but on a self-centered rationalization: "I'm going to forgive you because I assume that the pain is very bad" (42).

Edgar emerges as the most fully sketched of the minor characters. Like Sam, Edgar lives in a comfortable suburb, and by all indications he has been a forthright husband. He knows that the others dislike and mock his wife, which finally prompts a defense of his relationship. But what distinguishes Edgar is the quality of his awareness regarding Jo's and Sam's predicament, an awareness extending beyond his acknowledgment that the night "was your nice, average, desperate evening" (43). He emerges as the first character who addresses Jo's illness, but he immediately evades further discussion of her condition. He broaches the subject only much later when, significantly enough, Jo is absent.

Sam and Edgar's private dialogue progresses through two distinct stages, the first of which Albee laces with a series of virulent confrontations. Initially Edgar becomes annoyed, then angry, with Sam's sarcastic remarks. Pushed to emotional limits, Edgar suddenly explodes: "JESUS CHRIST, WHAT KIND OF HOUSE DO YOU RUN AROUND HERE?" (57). Clearly both men are angry, and long-suppressed emotions surface. However, their dialogue enters into a second stage, one characterized by a series of honest remarks. Progressing from tension to tonic, the two lower their defenses in a rare moment of rapport. Edgar offers assistance while Sam declines, reasoning that "nobody can help" (60).

But even here a sense of waste exists, since Edgar, in spite of his levelheadedness and sensitivity, fails to pinpoint the true source of Jo's suffering. Rather than talking with Jo about her illness and behavior, Edgar chooses to talk with Sam. Further, his remarks suggest that he is unable or unwilling to understand Jo's actions and the

PUBLIC ISSUES, PRIVATE TENSIONS

motives that fuel her outbursts. For a well-man-
nered, rational Edgar, Jo's outbursts are both embarrassing and unacceptable. His concern, it
seems, is not so much with Jo as it is with her
behavior, with her maintaining a civil, respectable
disposition. Albee heightens the sense of waste
since the audience expects more from Edgar. The
quality of Edgar's perceptions, after all, appears
sharper, more refined than Fred's, Carol's, or
Lucinda's, and therefore the possibility for his
understanding Jo's plight seems greater. Like the
others, however, Edgar misunderstands the full
nature of Jo's suffering. Such misunderstanding
only accentuates the wasted potential for communication and love to surface during the evening's
encounters.

Both Lucinda and Edgar, accordingly, waste
their opportunities to speak honestly with Jo. Like
the others their egotistical responses finally prevent them from sharing warmth and love or, at
least, from distracting Jo from her suffering. Two
occurrences confirm this point. The first takes
places in act 2 after an offended Edgar recounts
how his virtues apparently embarrass Sam.
Lucinda responds in a characteristically self-centered reply: "We don't forget, Sam; we may forgive, but we don't forget" (139). Lucinda's statements reveal a selfishness that precludes any

genuine understanding of their friends' circumstances. Moreover, their inability to forget certain events negates their potential for authentic growth, for it now appears that they will always regard Jo and Sam with rigid, preconceived notions. The second incident confirming their self-absorbtion occurs near the end of the play when Edgar and Lucinda relinquish claims to friendship by abandoning Sam (150–51). Always interpreting experience from their own points of view, they are ultimately unable to perceive the needs of their lifelong companions. In the hour of Sam and Jo's collective need, they leave.

Against this backdrop of the waste and self-centeredness of the supporting cast Albee presents the barrenness of the lives of the play's central characters. On one level the evening represents for Jo and Sam merely another social gathering of friends. But on a deeper level the events of the evening bring out the essence of Jo and Sam's relationship. Their public and private responses reveal that their lives together have largely been wasted. Jo's imminent death makes such barrenness all the more disheartening. For her it appears too late to redeem what has been a good marriage, in part because her friends offer little support, and also because physical frailty and decay are overtaking her. For Sam even his wife's dying cannot

PUBLIC ISSUES, PRIVATE TENSIONS

dislocate his self-serving interests; frailty and decay, on a symbolic level, are overtaking him. By the close of the drama we learn that their respective "reality needs," as Albee calls them,[5] do at times converge but more often remain at cross-purposes. Through the course of the play Albee suggests that Jo yearns for love and understanding, desires which Sam apparently cannot fulfill. Waste for this couple stems, not from Jo's physical deterioration and inevitable death, but from a crucial breakdown in communication between man and woman, from an inability to salvage qualitatively what scant time remains for Jo.

For Jo, an attractive and perspicacious woman, the gathering of friends for an evening of games and drink seems more bothersome than soothing. Moments into the play she voices her displeasure, expressing both her boredom and disgust with their presence and games (21). Her friends, respecting though not really understanding her predicament, uphold social appearance, either overlooking or enduring her remarks. But their well-meaning, if awkward, responses only exacerbate Jo's condition. Throughout the first act Albee presents Jo as one who vents her frustrations, berating longtime friends one moment, her husband the next. She displays little patience for Fred, who she calls "a reactionary, Nixon-loving fag baiter" (50), though she accepts Carol. The unassertive, complacent Lucinda riles Jo; she tolerates more than enjoys Edgar; and, while she loves her husband, ridicule overshadows her care for him. Frustrated by their unwillingness or inability to understand the real source of her suffering, Jo lashes out at everyone, taking comfort in aggressive verbal assaults. Albee portrays her friends, in turn, as failing to comprehend the underlying reasons for her actions, for they think that they must bear with Jo because she is, after all, ill. This is why June Schlueter suggests that in act 1 "we simply accept Jo as a somewhat obnoxious but pitiful woman who, unlike the others, has an excuse for her nastiness."[6]

Sam plays peacemaker in act 1. In trying to placate and make amends for Jo's brusque behavior, he continually explains and clarifies, attempting to smooth over social rough spots. A handsome forty-year-old, Sam mainly concerns himself with tactfully sustaining social appearances. As Jo sarcastically confides in one of her asides to the audience, "Sam's a real egalitarian; Sam pretends to like everyone equally" (28). In his efforts to please everybody, however, Sam ends up angering his guests and, more importantly, alienating himself from Jo.

Significantly, only at the end of act 1 do Jo and

PUBLIC ISSUES, PRIVATE TENSIONS

Sam communicate as if they are truly married. Here husband and wife attend to each other, talking and touching with a sense of commitment behind their deeds. In their rare moment of rapport there exists a still rarer expression, in this play, of genuine commitment. The tonal quality of the closing scene of act 1 is reminiscent of the rare loving expressions between George and Martha in *Who's Afraid of Virginia Woolf?* Significantly, during this unique time when Sam displays authentic affection for Jo, she willingly capitulates, relishing the expression of love that has been too long repressed:

> Jo: (*Instinctively, they run to each other and embrace*): Oh, my Sam, my Sam! I'd marry you in a minute! *Sam (Picks her up in his arms*): Shhh, shhh, shhh, shhh (70).

If Sam offers compassionate assistance, then Jo gladly receives it. Moreover, at this juncture Sam is presented as one still in control; it is still his house and Jo remains within his influence.

And yet and yet. The closing moments of act 1 also anticipate Sam's ultimately wasteful stance toward living. For example, he reasons that, as Jo dies, he must respond to the loss by holding "on to the object we're losing" (61). Reflecting on the meaning of her death, Sam seems unable to accept the reality of nonbeing. He clings selfishly to Jo "the object" to the extent that she becomes spiritually manacled. Importantly enough, the period in which Jo is most free in the play occurs when Sam is physically bound with a rope. The sense of waste becomes accentuated by his inability to distinguish between different forms of bondage—the kind Jo experiences versus the kind he endures. And the psychological damage caused by Sam's refusal to allow Jo or himself, in Albee's words, to "exhibit too much 'relatable' pain, psychologically"[7] fosters a profound sense of estrangement. In this light Sam does as much damage to the relationship as does Jo's physical disease. He reacts with hostility when shackled, just as Jo in act 1 reacts with hostility when symbolically shackled. Sam, like his friends, clings to "the object" he is losing because he can neither face up to nor comprehend death. He even appears emotionally paralyzed at times; Jo howls in agony while Sam stands and watches, unable to react on any level (51). Soon after, she talks about the illness, only to meet with Sam's evasions: "We just can't talk about it, it's that simple. [. . .] No. No, I don't want to hear them [Jo's report on two medical theories, one of which seems to be that of Kübler-Ross]" (68). Like so many Albee characters Sam avoids confronting painful truths.

PUBLIC ISSUES, PRIVATE TENSIONS

In the end the evening of drinks and games satisfies Sam's desires more than it soothes Jo's pains. At best the evening simply represents a distraction from her suffering and from his inability to confront directly the reality of her dying. Sam translates Jo's misery into how he must endure such pain. Obviously Sam's needs bear little on what Jo requires. Since Sam cannot or will not provide succor and since her mother has yet to help, she takes comfort in her aggressive verbal assaults.[8]

Jo and especially Sam are in many ways a suitable nucleus for the society which has gathered around them, reflecting as they do so many of its values. However, as has already been noted, act 2 disrupts the social order which Albee so carefully established in the first part of the play. In what might loosely be called a borrowing of the Romance device of the outsider whose entrance serves as a simultaneous threat to order and a call to adventure, Albee shatters the self-congratulation and complacency of the first act through the introduction of the outsiders, Elizabeth and Oscar. Functioning much like the White Rabbit who disrupts the well-established order of Alice's Victorian environs, the two strangers in *The Lady from Dubuque* lead a disbelieving Sam into a wonderland where the laws of time and space and logic established in the first part of the play are no longer in force, a world in which Elizabeth from New Jersey can be Jo's mother from Dubuque.

As denizens of the world beyond the tightly circumscribed realm of Sam and Jo's living room, Elizabeth and Oscar are markedly different from the regular habitúes of the house. Elizabeth is a stylish, elegant woman, and much of her stunning presence emerges from two contrasts. First, she looks markedly different from the other characters—patrician, eloquent, and a world traveler, radiating an air of mystery and sophistication. Her deportment acts as a counterpoint to the more common and at times raucous behavior of the other characters. Second, Elizabeth subverts the audience's as well as the other characters' expectations regarding her actual identity. That is, throughout the first act Jo's mother is described as a small, thin woman with "furtive blue eyes" and "pale hair, tinted pink, balding a little" (20). With stylish hat and fur cloak, Elizabeth hardly resembles Sam's description of his mother-in-law and emerges as anything but the less-cultured woman that her hometown title/name suggested to the New York critics. Coupled with Oscar, her black confidant, who is as debonair and composed as she

PUBLIC ISSUES, PRIVATE TENSIONS

is urbane and commanding, Elizabeth is set to usurp Sam's authority.

That usurpation is achieved by the making over of Sam's world into an abstract looking-glass world where everything is made over or reversed. Thus just as act 1 opens with a series of questions, Albee again uses this technique at the outset of the second act. Sam is quite serious in his exchange with the intruders, and this question-and-answer scene clearly mirrors the game of Twenty Questions which Sam delighted in playing the night before, much to his discomfort now. Fixed on Elizabeth and Oscar, Sam relentlessly probes, as his friends had regarding his identity in the game of Twenty Questions.

When Jo correctly guesses his identity in Twenty Questions, Sam sulks, rationalizing that she did not play his game fairly. These early moments are important in two respects. First, as the guessing game in act 1 was not, according to Sam, fairly played, so the real-life game in act 2, from Sam's point of view, will not be fairly played. Second, as Sam fails to handle defeat maturely in a simple quessing game, so he will fail later to handle defeat maturely in the most serious game of his life: when Jo necessarily separates from his world. This foreshadowing of Sam's weakness of character and ultimate loss of control also surfaces in his offhand confession that he dislikes Jo's mother (20). Sam, outwardly the one who enjoys everybody's company, emerges as the one who inwardly closes down to those who do not fit into the scheme of his desires. Finally, even the true identity of Elizabeth matters little to Sam because Albee presents him as rejecting anyone who unfavorably encroaches on his world. In Albee's presentation of Sam's world, there is no real sharing of the self with another individual. Consistently in act 2 Sam's immediate concern is not with healing but with prompting Jo to deny the identity of the nemesis who threatens his sense of propriety and order. By insistently pursuing his own rights, Sam spoils their last hours together.

Jo instinctively knows this. The intensity of her sarcasm in act 1 is a measure of her loss. Her responses stem from an awareness of the impending loss of her own life as well as from the realization that her relationship with Sam has deteriorated into a nonmarriage. With the support of Elizabeth, the outsider, Jo is able to confirm and accept her husband's beliefs, beliefs which are emotionally understandable in context but which also preserve their nonmarriage. Thus, Elizabeth and Oscar allow Jo and force Sam to redefine their reality. And to redefine their relationship in authentic terms is to unmask the lack of love between them. As Elizabeth confides to Jo: "He wasn't happy with the way things are. He wanted everything back the way it never was" (132). Though nearly comatose in the above exchange, Jo nevertheless recognizes the truth of Elizabeth's statements.

Jo detects and is attracted to the truth and comfort afforded by Elizabeth and Oscar. From the outset Albee indicates that Jo is not satisfied, and one can locate the source of much of her dissatisfaction in her confession that her mother never helped during the illness (18). Elizabeth's announcement that she is Jo's mother clearly establishes her as a crucial figure in Jo's world. But her true identity is irrelevant. The others are confused by this; Sam refuses to accept it; but whether or not Elizabeth is Jo's mother is subordinated to the role she plays, to the comfort she provides, and to the love she shares. The audience knows that Elizabeth is not Jo's mother, and a clearheaded Jo would surely know it too.

But Jo is dying. Her rational faculties, clouded by pain-dampening drugs and her body's decay, give way to emotional needs, needs that Elizabeth and Oscar satisfy. Albee's imagery gives shape to Jo's present state of being. In contrast to her remarks in act 1, her responses in act 2 are described as being "timid" (117), "dreamy" (127), "vague" (142), and "faint" (147), words which, in context, evoke deathlike images. As Jo nears death, her movements become hesitant, her utterances feeble. Like Sam, she is clothed in a sleeping gown as she begins her descent (116) toward the living room and her dying room.

Elisabeth Kübler-Ross explains that as one approaches death, one experiences an increasing need for sleep "very similar to that of the newborn child."[9] Jo not only lapses into longer periods of sleep, but the quality of her voice actually shifts into a childlike tone when Elizabeth cuddles her. Lured by the protection offered by the lady from Dubuque, Jo converses as "a little girl," giving herself over as a child to a mother. Albee's stage direction is emphatic: "*Finally, with tears and a great helpless smile, Jo rushes into Elizabeth's arms; their embrace is almost a tableau, so involved is it with pressing together*" (118).

If Elizabeth functions as a loving Mother-figure to Jo, she also represents, paradoxically, a less meaningful relationship. Jo necessarily prepares for death by gradually detaching herself from loved ones. Kübler-Ross suggests that it is a complex process, one usually met with misunderstanding; she observes with respect to a family's reactions to one who, like Jo, is on the brink of death, "They do not understand that a dying man who has found peace and acceptance in his death will have to separate himself, step by step, from his environment, including his most loved ones."[10] Jo finds herself in the midst of the final stages leading to her death when, near the end of the play, she is separating herself from Sam and her familiar surroundings.[11] Elizabeth and Oscar provide a necessary compromise between the total involvement with living and the total cessation of existence. Like such otherworldly Romance guides they provide a pathway to a displaced world beyond or, at the least, to a different state of being. Throughout, Albee presents the process of Jo's transition in its full complexity.

In direct contrast to Jo's letting go of the world she has known, Sam tries to maintain the status quo by claiming "rights" to his dearest possessions: Jo and home. In the hour of Jo's need Sam appears unable to help because of his stubborn belief in "rights." He mistakenly thinks that he can lay claim to, and have control over, Jo's emotions. Like Peter's claim to the park bench in *The Zoo Story*, Sam's claim to his possessions reduces him to a pathetic figure, one who perceives Jo and home as bits of "property" (145). Sam contributes to his own fall by perceiving the world around him solely from his own point of view.

Sam interprets Jo's acceptance of Elizabeth and Oscar as a mark of rejection and loss of control. For now he must abdicate his power, his possessions, his "rights." Oscar now dresses like Sam, utters some of Sam's previous lines, and, indeed, assumes Sam's former role as both protector and comforter. Elizabeth and Oscar create an illusion that assuages Jo's suffering, which Sam finally realizes. Sam's responses, of course, are understandable: Albee undermines Sam's reality by creating a fun-house mirror, a set in which all action is distorted. Perhaps Sam is not as selfish as he is human. However, in a final, desperate effort to communicate with his wife, Sam still does not fully comfort her. Despite Jo's pleas, Sam reverts to defining reality from his own reference point. Declaring that he is "not any part of" Jo's world any more (156) and asserting that it is he who is "dying" (155), Sam assures both Jo and himself of a wasted life together.

In several of Albee's plays the characters come to realize the possibility for spiritual regeneration. This motif has been seen in *The Zoo Story*, *Who's Afraid of Virginia Woolf?* and *Seascape*. However, such is not the case in *The Lady from Dubuque* because the characters remain incapable of seeking out a new understanding of the public and private self. Fred and Carol, with Edgar and Lucinda, retreat into their familiar habits, unchanged or only embittered by their recent experience. Elizabeth and Oscar, probably messengers of death, perform their duty and, with Jo's death, will simply take leave. Sam—unlike Peter in *The Zoo Story*, George and Martha in *Who's Afraid of Virginia Woolf?* or even Charlie in *Seascape*—learns little about love. He sees the help Elizabeth and Oscar give Jo but quickly loses sight of that comfort and returns to his self-centeredness. With his guests he remains as dead as the Romulus and Remus figures in the game of Twenty Questions. They have long conducted themselves as if they were "the very dead; who hear nothing; who remember nothing; who are nothing" (138).

Here, then, lies the irony of the drama. As in *All Over*, death is a ubiquitous force, encompassing not only Jo's literal death but also including figuratively the death of her friends and husband. All the physically healthy characters, with the exception of Elizabeth and Oscar, conduct themselves as if they were anesthetized to both their inner and outer worlds. Even the gray-colored interior of the setting appropriately captures the bleakness of the characters' inner existences. Finally, the presence of death gives Sam a chance to confront his real self and allows him the opportunity to participate in life honestly and compassionately. That Sam and the others apparently do not accept this kind of immersion into daily encounters confirms the wastefulness of their lives. If there is hope for a redemptive force, perhaps it lies with the audience, whose perceptions may be altered by the spectacle. As Albee has implied throughout his theater, that it is too late for his characters to change does not lessen the importance of self-awareness.

The Man Who Had Three Arms

After a controversial and unsuccessful adaptation of Vladimir Nabokov's *Lolita* (1981), Albee completed his next original work the following year, *The Man Who Had Three Arms*. In this play he addresses what he perceives as another form of waste: the collapse of the individual's moral nerve because of a public which demands a hero, despite the utter lack of substance within that hero.

The Man Who Had Three Arms, which opened 4 October 1982 at the Goodman Theatre in Chicago (it had its New York debut at the Lyceum in the spring of 1983), presents a hero savagely divided against his self and his world. Himself, the protagonist fixed behind the podium, emerges as one of Albee's more repulsive characters, for what strikes

PUBLIC ISSUES, PRIVATE TENSIONS

the viewer most forcibly about Himself is his stance toward the audience: he relentlessly lashes out at the theatergoer. Himself berates the audience in a desperate attempt to come to terms with the incubi haunting his soul: his undeserved fame and subsequent fall from undeserved stardom. After he mysteriously grew a third arm, the media and the public instantly elevated the man to celebrity status; but when the arm mysteriously disappeared, so went his fame, money, family—and a sense of self-control. Apparently the confluence of the public exposure and the private tensions within Himself explains his militant attitude toward the audience. His conspicuously aggressive attitude toward the audience only increases as he pathetically tries to come to terms with his predicament. In *The Zoo Story, Who's Afraid of Virginia Woolf?, A Delicate Balance*, and *Seascape* Albee created a certain objective distance between the actor and the audience; in *The Lady from Dubuque* the playwright diminished the actor/audience barrier, although the boundary remains clear. In *The Man Who Had Three Arms*, however, Albee banishes the fourth wall altogether. Himself lectures his invisible audience for two acts, presenting his own ethical conflicts directly to both an imagined and real audience. Himself launches a verbal attack, not on an unsuspecting Peter, a bewildered Nick and Honey, an anesthetized Tobias, or a retiring Charlie, but on his audience.

It is a Pirandellian audience, of course. That is, *The Man Who Had Three Arms* quickly establishes itself as a play whose words, gestures, character changes, repartee—its total content—transform the action into a metatheatrical experience. The play blatantly calls attention to its artificiality and deliberately makes the spectator aware of the theatricality of the theater; it is a play which calls attention to its own language while simultaneously exposing the meaninglessness of that language. Characters suddenly become different people. Himself also takes on multiple roles, but in another way: he is an actor within the play but also becomes the dramatist of the play, acting and writing his own pathetic script as he lectures the audience. The interplay of truth and illusion, the subversive influence of the text on the stage action, the banishing of the actor/audience barrier—these are the kinds of dramatic innovations Pirandello pioneered and which, in *The Man Who Had Three Arms*, Albee employs. The audience, then, is both the imaginary group of listeners attending the "Man on Man" lecture series and the actual theatergoer or reader. And this give-and-take between the actor and the spectator explains why, except for the Man and the Woman, whose repartee with

Himself is minimal, the actual audience becomes central participants in the drama.

The largely negative critical reception of the play may be understandable.[12] In the play's antimimetic texture, its alleged autobiographical nature (which does not make sense; the script makes it quite clear that the play is not autobiographical) and Himself's adamantine monologue of cruelty, critics found little to praise. Further, within the play's two-act structure, as Beckett scholar Vivian Mercier would say, nothing happens, twice. But what does occur—Himself's hostile account of his sudden rise to the top of fortune's wheel and his pathetic descent to the bottom of fortune's wheel—embodies Albee's thematic concerns.

Albee's Pirandellianism informs the play. The stage directions, for instance, signal the multiple roles the Man and the Woman will assume, allowing them to complement or disagree with Himself's narrative. At one point the Man and the Woman become, respectively, a physician and a nurse, aiding Himself's account of the medical world's reaction to his third appendage. Earlier, when Himself mocks the Catholic Church, the Man suddenly appears as a priest and accuses the speaker, "You are a freak of nature."[13] Also, like Pirandello before him, Albee embellishes scenes with a deliberate self-consciousness, as evident when, for example, the Man and the Woman call attention to the rhetorical gallantries—and artificiality—of their introductory exchange:

> *Woman*: . . . Dear friends, we *have* been fortunate over the years, being witness, as we have, to those who have made our history and shaped our culture, men and women whose accomplishments have wreaked their order on our havoc.
> *Man*: Oh! What a very nice phrase!
> *Woman*: (*Genuinely pleased*): Thank you, *thank* you! (*To her notes again*) . . . their order on our havoc and identified our reality by creating it for us.
> *Man*: Even better! (*Begins applauding*) My goodness.

Albee's Pirandellian technique, one also employed in *The Lady from Dubuque*, functions on two important levels. First, such a technique invites the audience to question its willing suspension of disbelief. By calling attention to the very nature of theatricality, Albee experiments with the illusion of dramatic mimesis, challenging traditional responses to the theater. *The Man Who Had Three Arms* testifies to Albee's willingness to examine, in C. W. E. Bigsby's words, "the nature of theatrical experiment" and his refusal "to accept conventional notions of theatrical propriety."[14] Second, like *Six Characters in Search of an Author*, *The Man Who Had Three Arms* forces the audience to break

PUBLIC ISSUES, PRIVATE TENSIONS

down the barrier between itself and the actors. However, in *The Man Who Had Three Arms*, Albee minimizes the barrier radically, involving the audience directly as participants throughout the action. At one point Himself talks to the audience, with the stage directions and dialogue suggesting the intimacy between the actor and spectator. Note the freedom within the script Albee provides in the exchange:

(*To someone in the front*): Do you remember what I said? Before we broke? Remember I said that if you came upon me sobbing in a corner, not to disturb? That it was a way I had and not to worry? Do you remember? (*Note: If the person says "yes," say: "You do!" If person says "no," say: "You don't!" If person fails to respond, wing it, choosing what you like*)

Albee does not direct Himself to start fighting with the actual audience, as Julian Beck had members of the Living Theatre do with his audience. Still, Albee creates an overly aggressive text, expanding the boundaries of theater as collective, communal spectacle. Albee discussed this point, observing the relatedness of the actors and audience within his theory of drama:

I don't like the audience as voyeur, the audience as passive spectator. I want the audience as participant. In that sense, I agree with Artaud: that sometimes we should literally draw blood. I am very fond of doing that because voyeurism in the theater lets people off the hook. *The Man Who Had Three Arms* is a specific attempt to do this. It is an act of aggression. It's probably the most violent play I've written.[15]

The play's fictional and actual audience, for better or worse, stands as the recipient of the violence.

Himself puts into concrete voice Albee's Artaudian dramatic theory. By drawing "blood," Himself supports the use of cruelty as a means of purging oneself of demons, of effecting a sense of catharsis, two factors which seem germane to Artaud's theater of cruelty.[16] Moments into the play Himself chides the audience, but the sarcasm is quickly transformed into the opprobrious verbal assault:

(*Looking across the front row*): Where is she? Where is she, I wonder; the lady, the girl, usually, who sits there in the front row, almost always, wherever, whenever I speak—not the *same* girl, woman, you understand, but of a certain type: plain, more than a little overweight, smock top, jeans, sandals, dirty toenails—sits there in the front row, and, as I lecture, *try* to lecture, try to fill you in, so to speak, make you understand, sits there and runs her tongue around her open mouth, like this, (*Demonstrates*) hand in her crotch, likely as not, bitten fingers, lascivious, obscene, does it over and over, all through my lec-

PUBLIC ISSUES, PRIVATE TENSIONS

ture, my expiation, my sad, sad tale, unnerves me,
bores, finally wearies me with her longing.

Act 2 begins with a tale that escalates Himself's
attack on the audience. Claiming a female journal-
ist hounded him during intermission, Himself
physically assaulted her, although Albee presents
the account ambiguously enough that the viewer is
never sure of its occurrence:

"You're good," she said, "you're really good." There
was a loathing to it, a condemnation that I dare be
articulate, coherent. "You're really good." "So are
you," I said. "You've got balls."

The energy of the hatred here, the mutual rage and
revulsion was such that, had we fucked, we would
have shaken the earth with our cries and thumps and
snarls and curses: a crashing around of Gods—
chewed nipples, bleeding streaks along the back. Had
we fucked. . . Oh, Jesus! what issue! *But* . . . but the
only issue was the issue of me, the . . . dismemberment of me. "You've got balls!" I said. And I crashed
my hand into her crotch like a goosing twelve-year-
old. "Get your hands off me," she said. "Get your
filthy hands off me." I withdrew my hand: it had hit
rock. "If you'll excuse me," she said, ice, shoving past
me. She *is* an impressive lady.

In his monologue of cruelty, then, Himself not
only chronicles the growth of his third arm and its
enervating effect on his world but implicates the

audience for contributing to his present condition. To be sure, his sudden fame had its positive points: he hobnobbed with British royalty: earned $25,000 an hour for public appearances; visited the White House; starred in ticker-tape parades; graced the covers of *People, Newsweek,* and *Time*; in brief, Himself became "the most famous man in the world." But the public, people like the omnipresent journalist he (may have) attacked, the fame, the wealth conspire, according to Himself, to undermine his sense of self-balance. Unable to deal with the decadence of celebrityhood, Himself loses sight of objective reality: his marriage dissolves; his own agent hornswoggles him; and after his mysterious arm disappears, the public discards him. By the time the play begins, Himself, once a freakish cultural icon, appears as a grotesque figure groveling to reorder his world. That is why he stands as a last-minute substitute speaker in this play, his last pathetic connection with a public he both needs and abhors.

On a thematic level *The Man Who Had Three Arms* thus exposes the monstrous effects of stardom on the individual's spirit. The play addresses "contemporary America's almost ghoulish need for culture heroes."[17] Within this context the public and the sycophants accentuate Himself's internal as well as external freakishness, canonizing him one moment, abandoning him the next, even though by his own admission he has no talent, has done nothing exemplary to achieve social accolades. As the third arm dissipates, so Himself's fame diminishes, reducing him to a pathetic figure consumed with self-pity. Like the unnamed hero in Pirandello's *When One Is Somebody*, Himself becomes a prisoner completely trapped within his (post)celebrityhood. In Albee's own assessment, the play thematically charts "the specifically American thing called 'hype': the creation of celebrity. The play is about the creation of celebrity and the destruction of celebrityhood, because his third arm starts going away. . . . So *The Man Who Had Three Arms* is about that particular kind of hype and celebrity: undeserved, unearned, and how we need it and how we destroy the person once we created him."[18]

Albee explores the corrupting and transitory effect of celebrityhood on the Great, the near-Great, and the pseudo-Great. On top of fortune's wheel one moment, relegated to the bottom the next moment, Himself experiences spiritual as well as financial bankruptcy. This explains why near the close of the play he specifically reflects on the loss of his self. Himself's hostility toward the audience measures the intensity of such loss. His anger, his directly involving the audience in his world, is apparently his form of expiation. Disassociated from his self and the other, the hurlyburly of his life now producing a new form of freakishness, Himself closes the play with a loving plea to stay, a hateful cry to leave, a pitiful gesture to understand. Throwing over the podium, Himself thus begs:

No one leaves until you apologize to me!! I want an apology for all the years!! For all the humiliation!! (*Sudden change of tone; abrupt realization of futility; a great weariness*) Nah! You don't owe me anything. Get out of here! Leave me alone! Leave me alone! (*Curtain starts; Himself notices*) (*Off*) No! Don't do that! Don't leave me alone! (*Out*) Stay with me. Don't . . . leave me alone! Don't leave me! Don't . . . leave me alone. (*Curtain completes itself*)

The ambivalence of Himself's closing lines reflects Albee's larger thematic concerns in the play. Himself does not wish to banish all people and institutions who have exacerbated his freakishness. Rather, he insists, without success, that those people and institutions not dismiss the private individual beneath the public façade. Himself's aggressive assault on the audience belies his inner need for sympathetic understanding of

PUBLIC ISSUES, PRIVATE TENSIONS

his humanness. It is a plea to be recognized as an individual, one consigned to an ordinary existence:

(*Out; pleading alternating with hatred*) I'm no different from you; I'm just like everyone you know; you love *them*: you love *me*. Stop treating me like a freak! I am *not* a freak! I am *you*! I have always *been* you! I am YOU!!! Stop looking at me!! Like that!!

Himself's social devoir seems so irreverent, his angry monody so relentless, of course, that he can never gain the audience's sympathy. In terms of psychology and motivations, Himself never earns the audience's compassion. The theatergoer could empathize with, say, a Jerry or a George and Martha, but one seems unable to muster much empathy for Himself. Hence Albee's efforts to involve the audience as a way to alter its perceptions about the individual's public and private worlds undercuts itself.

Many of Albee's heroes protest honestly—the existentialists would say authentically—against an absurd cosmos. Himself protests against a commercialized universe that divests him of self-freedom, understanding, and love. And Albee implicates the audience for its support of a Madison Avenue mentality promoting Himself's entrapment. Himself represents the latest Albee hero who has the courage to face life without absurd illusions. As Albee remarked, ''The entire structure of what happens to Himself is based totally on absurdity; and it is precisely the absurdity that he's railing against.''[19]

In theory and structure, in language and theme, *The Man Who Had Three Arms* boldly attempts to extend the conventions of the contemporary theater. The play stands as testimony to Albee's ongoing willingness to experiment with text and performance, without regard to commercial pressures. Albee certainly succeeds in fulfilling one of his central goals of drama: to involve the audience as active participants. However, the play does not sustain the dramaturgic burdens the author places on it. *The Man Who Had Three Arms* does not shock the audience into the self-awareness that we sense at the closure of *The Zoo Story*; the play does not produce the catharsis we experience at the climax of *Who's Afraid of Virginia Woolf? The Man Who Had Three Arms* is at its best in a thematic context, although in dramatic terms Himself's monologue of cruelty is less than satisfying. Significantly enough, however, the play, like his experimental *Finding The Sun*,[20] once again indicates that Albee is always eager to restructure his stage according to the demands of his performance instincts.

PUBLIC ISSUES, PRIVATE TENSIONS

Notes

1. Edward Albee, *The Lady from Dubuque* (New York: Atheneum, 1980) 33. Page references within the text are to this edition.

2. Eugene O'Neill, *Anna Christie, The Emperor Jones, The Hairy Ape* (New York: Vintage, 1972) 172, 230–32.

3. Edward Albee, *A Delicate Balance* (New York: Atheneum, 1966) 80.

4. Edward Albee, *All Over* (New York: Atheneum, 1971) 19.

5. Matthew C. Roudané, "An Interview with Edward Albee," *Southern Humanities Review* 16 (1982): 40.

6. June Schlueter, "Is It 'All Over' for Edward Albee? *The Lady from Dubuque*," *Edward Albee: Planned Wilderness*, ed. Patricia De La Fuente (Edinburg, TX: Pan American University Press, 1980) 116.

7. Roudané 40.

8. See Elisabeth Kübler-Ross, *On Death and Dying* (New York: Macmillan, 1970) 50–57. According to Kübler-Ross, who Albee says influenced the composition of the play, the dying person progresses through various stages as he or she approaches death. The second stage appears when the patient is filled with "anger, rage, and resentment." This seems to account for Jo's capriciousness in act 1.

9. Kübler-Ross 112.

10. Kübler-Ross 170.

11. For Jo the anger of act 1 yields to the resignation of act 2. She realizes that she must lose friends, home, husband, and, finally, herself. Because of her awareness of death Sam and friends become less important. They interpret this as a mark of disrespect or nonlove; it is, according to Kübler-Ross, the mark of a psychological process, *decathexis*, or separation, which Jo necessarily experiences. See Kübler-Ross 119, 170, 176.

12. For a survey of the Chicago and New York reviews of the play see Matthew C. Roudané, "A Monologue of Cruelty: Edward Albee's *The Man Who Had Three Arms*," *Critical Essays on Edward Albee* ed. Philip C. Kolin and J. Madison Davis (Boston: Hall, 1986) 191–92.

13. Edward Albee, *The Man Who Had Three Arms* (New York: Atheneum, forthcoming). I used the galley proofs of the play, and I

am extremely grateful to Mr. Albee for giving me access to the play long before its publication in book form.

14. Introduction, *Edward Albee*, ed. C. W. E. Bigsby (Englewood Cliffs, NJ: Prentice-Hall, 1975) 8–9.

15. Matthew C. Roudané, "Albee on Albee," *RE: Artes Liberales* 10 (1984): 1–2.

16. See Antonin Artaud, *The Theater and Its Double*, trans. Mary Caroline Richards (New York: Grove, 1958); for further discussions of Artaud's theories and the audience response which may prove useful in understanding Albee's play, see Peter L. Podol, "Contradictions and Dualities in Artaud and Artaudian Theater: *The Conquest of Mexico* and the Conquest of Peru," *Modern Drama* 26 (1983): 518–27; and Una Chaudhuri, "The Spectator in Drama/Drama in the Spectator," *Modern Drama* 27 (1984): 281–98.

17. Thomas P. Adler, "*The Man Who Had Three Arms*," *Theatre Journal* 35 (1983): 124.

18. Roudané, "Albee on Albee" 2.

19. Matthew C. Roudané, "A Playwright Speaks: An Interview with Edward Albee," Kolin and Davis 198.

20. For a detailed review of Albee's experimentation see Linda Ben-Zvi, "*Finding The Sun*," *Theatre Journal* 36 (1984): 102–03.

CONCLUSION

If I were a pessimist I wouldn't bother to write. Writing, itself, taking the trouble, communicating with your fellow human being is valuable, that's an act of optimism. There's a positive force within the struggle. Serious plays are unpleasant in one way or another, and my plays examine people who are not living their lives fully, dangerously, properly.

Edward Albee, 1985

Poetry, Robert Frost writes, "ends in a clarification of life—not necessarily a great clarification, such as sects or cults are founded on, but in a momentary stay against confusion."[1] Perhaps Albee's most important contribution to contemporary American literature lies in his ability to present on stage the kind of clarification Frost envisioned. When he is at his best, Albee produces in certain characters and, ideally, in the audience "a momentary stay against confusion," a still point in the messy business of living that paves the way for the possibility of existing with a heightened sense of self-responsibility. Heated repartee, sexual tensions, indecisiveness, death, a preoccupation with vital lies, a withdrawal from meaningful human encounters, indifference—these are the issues that Albee mines, but not from the position of a nihilist. Rather, Albee explores these issues because they can trigger in his plays catharsis, existential growth, and an ultimately affirmative, life-giving experience for his characters and audiences. He pinpoints the value of writing this kind of drama:

Many people at the colleges I visit ask me over and again, "Why do you ask such tough questions and why do your plays seem so difficult or depressing?" Or "Why don't you write happy plays?" About what, happy problems? But I keep reminding them that drama is an attempt to make things better. Drama is a mirror held up to them to show the way they do behave and how they don't behave that way any longer. If people are willing to be aided in the search for total consciousness by not only drama but all the arts—music and painting and all the other arts give a unique sense of order—then art is life-giving. Art gives shape to life; it increases consciousness.[2]

To understand the role of death in Albee's theater, paradoxically enough, is to understand the compassion, the affirmation, the optimism of his world view. The plays are death-saturated because the presence of death, once internalized, shapes the quality of human existence. The playwright em-

CONCLUSION

phatically states his views with respect to his preoccupation with death:

As opposed to the slaughter in Shakespeare, the tuberculosis and consumption in Chekhov, the death-in-life in Beckett? Is that what you mean? There are only a few significant things to write about: life and death; and the fact that people avoid thinking about death—and about *living*. I think we should always live with the consciousness of death. How else can we possibly participate in living life fully?[3]

Since *The Zoo Story*, Albee has always brought such an attitude to the design of each new play.

Albee dominated the American stage during the 1960s. However, his later works, despite whatever merits they have, do not compare well with his 1960s compositions. His language, which once so engaged audiences, has become more mannered, abstract, more difficult to apprehend in text or performance. Many of the later plays, which may seem more like daring, unfinished experiments than polished plays, cannot always sustain the dramaturgic burdens Albee places on them. Some of the later plays, many critics feel, simply repeat what have become outworn themes. Adding to Albee's decline in reputation are the newer voices that have eclipsed him. Wendy Wasserstein's humor, David Mamet's elided street dialogue, Sam Shepard's myth-making, for instance, presently stir more critical attention. On the other hand, Albee continues to display an acute sensitivity to European dramatic tradition; the courage to experiment with the essence of theater; and to restructure the stage in the spirit of a dramatic innovator. He refuses to repeat old formulas, to direct safe productions that might raise his reputation in commercial terms. For him this would compromise his serious commitment to produce original theater.

Albee remains one of the most influential and controversial American dramatists. He is responsible for introducing European dramatic influences within a uniquely American context; for revitalizing the American theater through clever dialogue; for exploring the human soulscape in images as powerful as those of O'Neill, Williams, and Miller in their respective masterworks. In brief, Albee must be credited with reinventing the American stage at a time when its originality and quality seemed to be fading. He continues to be a major spokesperson for the moral seriousness of American theater. Above all, he has the artistic instinct, even arrogance, to stage significant, universal public issues and private tensions of the individual and a culture thinking in front of themselves.

CONCLUSION

Notes

1. Robert Frost, *Complete Poems of Robert Frost* (New York: Holt, Rinehart, 1964) vi.

2. Matthew C. Roudané, "A Playwright Speaks: An Interview with Edward Albee," *Critical Essays on Edward Albee*, ed. Philip C. Kolin and J. Madison Davis (Boston: Hall, 1986) 194–95.

3. Roudané 195.

BIBLIOGRAPHY

Published Plays by Albee

"Schism." *Choate Literary Magazine* 32 (1946): 87–110.

The Zoo Story and The American Dream. New York: Signet, 1960.

The Zoo Story, The Death of Bessie Smith, The Sandbox. New York: Coward-McCann, 1960.

The American Dream. New York: Coward-McCann, 1961.

Who's Afraid of Virginia Woolf? New York: Atheneum, 1962; London: Jonathan Cape, 1964.

The Sandbox, The Death of Bessie Smith, with Fam and Yam. New York: New American Library, 1963.

Tiny Alice. New York: Atheneum, 1965; London: Jonathan Cape, 1966.

A Delicate Balance. New York: Atheneum, 1966; London: Jonathan Cape, 1968.

Box and Quotations from Chairman Mao Tse-Tung. New York: Atheneum, 1969; London: Jonathan Cape, 1970.

All Over. New York: Atheneum, 1971.

Seascape. New York: Atheneum, 1975; London: Jonathan Cape, 1976.

Counting the Ways and Listening. New York: Atheneum, 1977.

The Lady from Dubuque. New York: Atheneum, 1980.

The Plays, Vol. 1. New York: Coward, McCann, and Geoghegan, 1981.

The Plays, Vol. 2. New York: Atheneum, 1983.

The Plays, Vol. 3. New York: Atheneum, 1983.

The Plays, Vol. 4. New York: Atheneum, 1984.

The Man Who Had Three Arms. New York: Atheneum, forthcoming [1987].

Finding the Sun, in progress.

Adaptations

The Ballad of the Sad Cafe. Boston: Houghton Mifflin; New York:

BIBLIOGRAPHY

Atheneum, 1963. Adaptation of Carson McCullers's novella of the same name.

Malcolm. New York: Atheneum, 1966; London: Jonathan Cape, 1967. Adaptation of James Purdy's novel *Malcolm.*

Breakfast at Tiffany's. Music by Bob Merrill. Produced in Philadelphia, 1966. Musical adaptation of Truman Capote's *Breakfast at Tiffany's.*

Everything in the Garden. New York: Atheneum, 1968. Adaptation of Giles Cooper's play of the same name.

Lolita. New York: Dramatists Play Service, 1984. Adaptation of Vladimir Nabokov's novel *Lolita.*

Other: *Bartleby.* Libretto adaptation of Herman Melville's short story (January 1961). *Envy.* Part of Nagel Jackson's *Faustus in Hell* (January 1985).

Unpublished Plays

The following are unpublished and unperformed plays written by Albee. The manuscripts are held at the New York Public Library at Lincoln Center and may be seen only after Albee himself grants special permission. They are not intended for performance. (This information is from C. W. E. Bigsby, *Edward Albee: Bibliography, Biography, Playography,* Theatre Checklist No. 22 [London: TQ Publications, 1980] 4–6.)

The City of People (1949). 177-page manuscript.

Untitled Play (perhaps *In a Quiet Room*; 1949). 34-page manuscript.

Ye Watchers and Ye Lonely Ones (1951).

The Invalid (1952). 18-page manuscript.

The Making of a Saint (1953–54). 76-page manuscript.

The Ice Age (undated). 35-page manuscript.

An End to Summer (undated). 40-page manuscript.

BIBLIOGRAPHY

Untitled Play (perhaps *The Recruit*; undated). 9-page manuscript.
Untitled Opera (perhaps *Hatchet, Hatchet*; undated).

Short Stories by Albee
"L'Apres-midi d'un faune." *Choate Literary Magazine* 21 (1944):
43–44.
"Empty Tea." *Choate Literary Magazine* 31 (1945): 53–59.
"A Place on the Water." *Choate Literary Magazine* 32 (1945):
15–18.
"Well, It's Like This." *Choate Literary Magazine* 32 (1945): 31–34.
"Lady with an Umbrella." *Choate Literary Magazine* 32 (1946):
5–10.
"A Novel Beginning." *Esquire* 60 (1963): 59–60.

Poems by Albee
"Old Laughter." *Choate Literary Magazine* 31 (1944): 37–38.
"To a Gold Chain Philosopher at Luncheon." *Choate Literary
Magazine* 31 (1945): 34.
"To Whom It May Concern." *Choate Literary Magazine* 31
(1945): 61.
"Associations." *Choate Literary Magazine* 31 (1945): 15–16.
"Frustrations." *Choate Literary Magazine* 31 (1945): 60.
"Questions." *Choate Literary Magazine* 31 (1945): 81.
"Monologue," "The Atheist," and "Sonnet." *Choate Literary
Magazine* 32 (1945): 10.
"Reunion." *Choate Literary Magazine* 32 (1945): 71–72.
"Eighteen." *Kaleidograph* 17 (1945): 15.
"Interlude." *Choate Literary Magazine* 32 (1946): 29.
"To a Maniac." *Choate Literary Magazine* 32 (1946): 71.
"Nihilist." *Choate Literary Magazine* 32 (1946): 22.

BIBLIOGRAPHY

"Peaceable Kingdom, France." *New Yorker* 29 Dec. 1975: 34.

Articles by Albee

"Richard Strauss." *Choate Literary Magazine* 31 (1945): 87–93.

"Chaucer: The Legend of Phyllis." *Choate Literary Magazine* 32 (1945): 59–63.

"What's It About?—A Playwright Tries to Tell." *New York Herald Tribune Magazine*, "The Lively Arts" 22 Jan. 1961: 5.

"Which Theatre Is the Absurd One?" *New York Times Magazine* 25 Feb. 1962: 30–31, 64, 66.

"Some Notes on Non-Conformity." *Harper's Bazaar* Aug. 1962: 104.

"Carson McCullers—The Case of the Curious Magician." *Harper's Bazaar* Jan. 1963: 98.

Review of Lillian Ross's novel *Vertical and Horizontal*. *Village Voice* 11 July 1963: 1.

"Who's Afraid of the Truth?" *New York Times*, Sunday Drama Section 18 Aug. 1963: 1.

"Ad Libs on Theater." *Playbill* May 1965.

Review of Sam Shepard's *Icarus' Mother*. *Village Voice* 25 Nov. 1965: 19.

Introduction. *Three Plays by Noel Coward*. New York: Dell, 1965.

"Who Is James Purdy?" *New York Times*, Sunday Drama Section, 9 Jan. 1966: 1, 3.

"Creativity and Commitment." *Saturday Review*, 4 June 1966: 26.

"Judy Garland." *Double Exposure*. Ed. Roddy McDowell. New York: Delacorte, 1966: 198–199.

"Apartheid in the Theater." *New York Times*, Sunday Drama Section 30 July 1967: 1, 6.

"Albee Says 'No Thanks' to John Simon." *New York Times*, Sunday Drama Section 10 Sept. 1967: 1, 8.

BIBLIOGRAPHY

"The Decade of Engagement." *Saturday Review* 24 Jan. 1970: 19–20.
"The Future Belongs to Youth." *New York Times*, Sunday Drama Section 26 Nov. 1971: 1.
"Albeit." *The Off-Broadway Experience*. Ed. Howard Greenberger (Englewood Cliffs, NJ: Prentice-Hall, 1971): 52–62.
"Edward Albee on Louise Nevelson: The World Is Beginning to Resemble Her Art." *Art News* (1980): 99–101.
Foreword. *Dream Palaces*. By James Purdy. New York: Viking, 1980: vii–ix.

Secondary Sources

Selected Bibliographies
Amacher, Richard E., and Margaret Rule. *Edward Albee at Home and Abroad*. New York: AMS Press, 1973. Primary and secondary.
Bigsby, C. W. E. *Edward Albee: Bibliography, Biography, Playography*. Theatre Checklist No. 22. London: TQ Publications, 1980. Primary and secondary.
Giantvalley, Scott. *Edward Albee: A Reference Guide* (Boston: G. K. Hall, 1987). Secondary.
Green, Charles. *Edward Albee: An Annotated Bibliography, 1968–1977*. New York: AMS Press, 1980. Primary and secondary.
King, Kimball. *Ten Modern American Playwrights: An Annotated Bibliography*. New York: Garland, 1982. 1–108. Primary and secondary.
Kolin, Philip C. "A Classified Edward Albee Checklist," *Serif* 6 (1969): 16–32.
———. "A Supplementary Edward Albee Checklist." *Serif* 10 (1973): 28–39. Secondary.

BIBLIOGRAPHY

Books on Albee

Amacher, Richard E. *Edward Albee*. Rev. ed. Boston: Twayne, 1982. Careful explication of each play through *Lolita*; contains useful biographical background material and a discussion of Albee's dramatic theories.

Bigsby, C. W. E. *Albee*. Edinburgh: Oliver and Boyd, 1969. Identifies Albee's liberal humanistic concerns; by one of the world's leading Albee scholars.

———, ed. *Edward Albee*. Englewood Cliffs, NJ: Prentice-Hall, 1975. Provocative introduction and 21 essays, reviews, and interviews.

Braem, Helmut M. *Edward Albee*. Hannover, Germany: Velber Verlag, 1968. Useful European perspective; in German.

Cohn, Ruby. *Edward Albee*. Minneapolis: University of Minnesota Press, 1969. Excellent monograph on Albee.

Debusscher, Gilbert. *Edward Albee: Tradition and Renewal*. Trans. Anne D. Williams. Brussels: Center for American Studies, 1967. Discusses the European influence on Albee's aesthetic; concludes that Albee is a nihilist.

De La Fuente, Patricia, ed. *Edward Albee: Planned Wilderness: Interviews, Essays, and Bibliography*. Living Author Series 3. Edinburg, TX: Pan American University Press, 1980. Includes 8 essays, an interview, and a bibliography.

Hayman, Ronald. *Edward Albee*. New York: Ungar, 1971. Explicates each play.

Hirsch, Foster. *Who's Afraid of Edward Albee?* Berkeley: Creative Arts, 1978. Interprets the plays from a biographical viewpoint; discusses the influence of Albee's homosexuality on the characters.

Kerjan, Lillian. *Albee*. Paris: Seghers, 1971. In French.

———. *Le Théâtre d'Edward Albee*. Paris: Klincksieck, 1979. In French.

Kolin, Philip C., and J. Madison Davis, eds. *Critical Essays on*

204

BIBLIOGRAPHY

Edward Albee. Boston: Hall, 1986. The most impressive collection of essays on Albee to date. Includes 39 essays, interviews, reviews. Features comprehensive bibliographic essay on Albee scholarship.

McCarthy, Gerald. *Edward Albee*. London: Macmillan, 1985.

Paolucci, Anne. *From Tension to Tonic: The Plays of Edward Albee*. Carbondale: Southern Illinois University Press, 1972. Language is Albee's major contribution; one of the best studies on Albee; considers the existentialist dimension of the plays.

Rutenberg, Michael E. *Edward Albee: Playwright in Protest*. New York: Avon, 1969. Sees Albee as highly political writer whose plays are, above all, social protest works. Includes two interviews.

Schultz-Seitz, Ruth Eva. *Edward Albee, der Dichterphilosoph der Buhne*. Frankfurt am Main: Vittorio Klostermann, 1966. In German.

Stenz, Anita Marie. *Edward Albee: The Poet of Loss*. The Hague: Mouton, 1978. Argues that Albee challenges the buffers or illusions people create to shield themselves from reality. Stenz concentrates on the characters' psychologies in this solid study.

Wasserman, Julian N., ed. *Edward Albee: An Interview and Essays*. Lee Lecture Series, University of St. Thomas, Houston. Syracuse: Syracuse University Press, 1983. Includes lengthy interview with Albee and 8 essays.

Selected Interviews

"Albee." *New Yorker* 25 Mar. 1961: 30–32. Discusses *Zoo Story* and contains biographical data.

"Albee Revisited." *New Yorker* 19 Dec. 1964: 31–33. Discusses *Tiny Alice*.

Booth, John E. "Albee and Schneider Observe: 'Something's

BIBLIOGRAPHY

Stirring.'" *Theatre Arts* 45 (1961): 22–24, 78–79. Conversation with the man who directed many of Albee's earlier plays.

Brenner, Marie. "Tiny Montauk." *New York* 22 Aug. 1983: 13–15. Focuses on Albee's summer home; includes photograph.

Diehl, Digby. "Edward Albee." *Transatlantic Review* 13 (1963): 57–72. Discussion of Albee's world view, opinions about the audience, and the musicality of his plays; solid interview.

"Edward Albee." *New Yorker* 3 June 1974: 28–30. Discusses the civic function of theater.

Flanagan, William. "Interview with Edward Albee." *The Paris Review* 10 (1966): 93–121. Conversation with former roommate.

Gussow, Mel. "Albee: Odd Man In on Broadway." *Newsweek* 4 Feb. 1963: 49–52. Includes rare photo of Albee with his mother.

Kolin, Philip C., ed. *Conversations with Edward Albee*. Jackson: University Press of Mississippi, forthcoming [1988]. Will contain about twenty of the over eighty Albee interviews.

"Revisited." *New Yorker* 3 Mar. 1980: 29–31. Albee talks about *The Lady from Dubuque*.

Roudané, Matthew C. "An Interview with Edward Albee." *Southern Humanities Review* 16 (1982): 29–44. Albee discusses his central thematic concerns and dramatic theories.

———. "Albee on Albee." *RE: Artes Liberales* 10 (1984): 1–8. Discusses role of communication and *The Man Who Had Three Arms*.

———. "A Playwright Speaks: An Interview with Edward Albee." *in Critical Essays on Edward Albee*, ed. Philip C. Kolin and J. Madison Davis. Boston: Hall, 1986. 193–199. Albee discusses the affirmative nature of death in his plays, the importance of consciousness, and his world views.

BIBLIOGRAPHY

Wager, Walter, ed. *The Playwrights Speak*. New York: Delta, 1968. 25–67. A conversation with Albee.

Selected Articles and Chapters in Books on Albee

Adler, Thomas P. "Albee's *Virginia Woolf*: A Long Night's Journey into Day." *Educational Theatre Journal* 25 (1973): 66–70. Sees George's exorcism of the child as the replacing of one reality with another; Martha will depend on George's strength as a defense against her fear of the unknown.

———. "Albee's *Seascape*: Humanity at the Second Threshold." *Renascence* 31 (1979): 107–14. Sees *Seascape* as a reverse mirror image of *Delicate Balance*; identifies regenerative possibilities in *Seascape*.

———. "Edward Albee." *Critical Survey of Drama: English Language Series*, ed. Frank McGill. Englewood Cliffs, NJ: Salem Press, 1985. 11–23. An overview of the playwright's central themes and techniques. Concludes that Albee's aesthetic experiments reflect his thematic concern with the need for venturing into the unknown if there is to be any chance for growth.

Anderson, Mary Castiglie. "Staging the Unconscious: Edward Albee's *Tiny Alice*." *Renascence* 32 (1980): 178–92. Excellent study which seeks to explain the relationship of the ego, id, and superego as it pertains to the characters in the play.

Bernstein, Samuel. *The Strands Entwined: A New Direction in American Drama*. Boston: Northeastern University Press, 1980. Chapter on *Seascape*.

Bigsby, C. W. E. *A Critical Introduction to Twentieth-Century American Drama*. Vol. 2. New York. Cambridge University Press, 1984. One-third of the book is devoted to Albee; considers in detail Albee's early, unpublished material. Excellent study.

BIBLIOGRAPHY

Brustein, Robert. *Seasons of Discontent*. New York: Simon and Schuster, 1965. 26–49; 145–48; 155–58; 304–11.

———. "The Trashing of Edward Albee." *New Republic* 11 Apr. 1981: 27–28. Concedes Albee has become the raw flesh of the American theater but praises *Lolita*.

Coe, Richard M. "Beyond Absurdity: Albee's Awareness of Audience in *Tiny Alice*." *Modern Drama* 18 (1975): 371–83.

Cohn, Ruby. "Albee's *Box* and Ours." *Modern Drama* 14 (1971): 137–43. Examines the musicality of *Box and Quotations from Chairman Mao Tse-Tung*.

———. *Currents in Contemporary Drama*. Bloomington: Indiana University Press, 1969. Excellent focus on Albee's accusative dialogues; see 4, 6, 8–10, 20–21, 71–74, 84, 182–86, 247–50.

Copeland, Roger. "Should Edward Albee Call It Quits?" *Saturday Review* Feb. 1981: 28–31. Thinks Albee has exhausted his storehouse of metaphors.

Dutton, Richard. *Modern Tragicomedy and the British Tradition*. Norman: University of Oklahoma Press, 1986. Chapter on *Virginia Woolf*.

Egri, Peter. "European Origins and American Originality: The Case of Drama." *Zeitschrift für Anglistik und Amerikanistik* 29 (1981): 179–206. Excellent survey, written in English, of the European influence on Albee and others.

Esslin, Martin. *The Theatre of the Absurd*. Rev. ed. Woodstock, NY: Overlook Press, 1969. Calls Albee the first American dramatist to use successfully the techniques of the great European absurdists. See 266–70.

Fumerton, M. Patricia. "Verbal Prisons: The Language of Albee's *A Delicate Balance*." *English Studies in Canada* 7 (1981): 201–11. Argues that each character evades confronting reality by creating words to deflect authentic encounters.

Gabbard, Lucina P. "From O'Neill to Albee." *Modern Drama* 19

BIBLIOGRAPHY

(1976): 365–73. Places Albee in context of the development of American drama. Compares *The Hairy Ape* and *Zoo Story*.

———. "Albee's *Seascape*: An Adult Fairy Tale." *Modern Drama* 21 (1978): 307–17. Discusses archetypal elements and major symbols of the play.

———. "Edward Albee's Triptych on Abandonment." *Twentieth Century Literature* 28 (1982): 14–33. On *The Zoo Story*, *The Death of Bessie Smith*, and *Sandbox*; claims that Albee's social protest is rooted in the psychological trauma of abandonment.

———. "The Enigmatic *Tiny Alice*." *Journal of Evolutionary Psychology* 6 (1985): 73–86.

Grunnes, Dennis. "God and Albee: *Tiny Alice*." *Studies in American Drama 1945–Present*. 1 (1986): 61–71.

Hardy, Hathaway. "Edward Albee." *Architectural Digest* 39 (1982): 150–55. Provides a glimpse into Albee's homes.

Harris, James N. "Edward Albee and Maurice Maeterlinck: *All Over* as Symbolism." *Theatre Research Institute* 3 (1978): 200–08. Sees the play as a symbolist drama, one throwing light on Albee's existentialism; notes convincingly Maeterlinck's influence.

Kane, Leslie. *The Language of Silence: On the Unspoken and the Unspeakable in Modern Drama*. Rutherford, NJ: Fairleigh Dickinson University Press, 1984. Discusses Albee, especially *Zoo Story*, on 158–78.

Kauffmann, Stanley. "Edward Albee: All Over?" *Saturday Review* 15 Mar. 1980: 34–35. Claims Albee has depleted his dramatic resources.

Kolin, Philip C. "Bawdy Uses of *Et Cetera*." *American Speech* 58 (1983): 75–8. Discusses indelicate use of *et cetera* from Shakespeare to Albee; focuses on *Listening*.

Morrison, Kristin. "Pinter, Albee, and 'The Maiden in the

BIBLIOGRAPHY

Shark Pond.'" *American Imago* 35 (1978): 259–74. Discusses *Tiny Alice*.

Otten, Terry. *After Innocence: Visions of the Fall in Modern Literature*. Pittsburgh: Pittsburgh University Press, 1982. 174–91. On *Who's Afraid of Virginia Woolf?*

Paolucci, Anne. "Pirandello and the Waiting Stage of the Absurd (with Some Observations on a New 'Critical Language')." *Modern Drama* 23 (1980): 102–11. Useful remarks on how to see Albee's plays.

———. "Albee and the Restructuring of the Modern Stage." *Studies in American Drama, 1945–Present* 1 (1986): 3–23. Explains Albee's experiments with dramatic language and structure.

Porter, M. Gilbert. "Toby's Last Stand: The Evanescence of Commitment in *A Delicate Balance*." *Educational Theatre Journal* 31 (1979): 398–408. Tobias is seen as the center of the play; discusses the death-in-life existence the characters lead.

Robinson, Fred Miller. "Albee's Long Night's Journey into Day." *Modern Language Studies* 11 (1981): 25–32. Sees *A Delicate Balance* as a comedy of contemporary manners.

Rogoff, Gordon. "Albee and Mamet: The War of the Words." *Saturday Review* 2 Apr. 1977: 36–37. Discusses powerful language of both writers.

Roudané, Matthew C. "Animal Nature, Human Nature, and the Existentialist Imperative: Edward Albee's *Seascape*." *The Theatre Annual* 38 (1983): 31–47. Discusses the existential growth of the characters.

———. "Communication as Therapy in the Theater of Edward Albee." *Journal of Evolutionary Psychology* 6 (1985): 302–17. Discusses the cleansing value of honest communication in Albee, with a focus on *The Lady from Dubuque*.

BIBLIOGRAPHY

Sarotte, Georges M. "Edward Albee: Homosexual Playwright in Spite of Himself." *Like a Brother, Like a Lover: Male Homosexuality in the American Novel and Theatre From Herman Melville to James Baldwin*. Trans. Richard Miller. Garden City: Anchor, 1978. 134–49.

Schlueter, June. *Metafictional Characters in Modern Drama*. New York: Columbia University Press, 1979. 79–87. Excellent focus on *Who's Afraid of Virginia Woolf?*

Simard, Rodney. *Postmodern Drama: Contemporary Playwrights in America and Britain*. Lanham, MD: University Press of America, 1984. Places Albee within a postmodern dramatic aesthetic; very useful study. Analyses Albee 25–47.

Szilassy, Zoltan. *American Theater of the 1960s*. Carbondale: Southern Illinois University Press, 1986. Includes chapter on Albee; from the perspective of a Hungarian scholar.

INDEX

INDEX

INDEX

INDEX

INDEX

INDEX

INDEX

INDEX